MIND CHANGE

Changing The World One Mind At A Time

HEATHER MCKEAN

Copyright © 2019 Mind Change, LLC

Written by Heather McKean

Cover art by Kent McKean

McKean, Heather, 1976-
    Mind Change: Changing the World One Mind at a Time

Mind Change, LLC
PO Box 791377
Paia, HI 96779

ISBN: 978-0-578-51703-2
www.MindChange.com

To my clients…thank you for your trust, your perseverance and the belief you have in yourself. And thank you for allowing me to be a fellow traveler on your journey. I promise to always remain a student.

To my friends…thank you for your unfailing support, even when you didn't hear from me for months at a time.

To my children Cadence and Savannah…thank you for demanding my time, my energy and my attention even during deadlines. You absolutely deserve it!

To my husband…there are not enough pages in this book, or any book, to capture my gratitude for all that you are to me. You are my biggest fan, my fellow dreamer, my constant companion as I continue to choose the road less traveled. My editor, technical advisor, designer and coworker. You are my partner, my lover and my friend. I couldn't have completed this without your support and guidance.

To God…thank you for your patience with me as I endeavor to learn what love really is.

Those who cannot change their minds cannot change anything

George Bernard Shaw

Table Of Contents

INTRODUCTION

If you are an avid reader or just a person who values their time, you probably ask yourself a common question before reading or purchasing a book… "Will this book help me?" Over the years, I have read hundreds (if not thousands) of different kinds of books. I happen to like, as a rare and guilty pleasure, mystery novels of the "spooky" persuasion. Most commonly, Dean Koontz or Stephen King types of books. I'm quite picky about how I spend my time reading. I am even pickier when it comes to "Self-Help." I have read many and found that some are excellent, but some are what I like to call "fluff." "Fluff," in my definition, is a feel-good story that will make you smile but is very short on practical application or a new perspective. It's commonly a gentle re-hashing of a well-known concept or idea. I don't like "fluff." My time is valuable and, when I choose to read a self-improvement book, I want my life to change. So it stands to reason that if I like to read books that will change my life, I would want to write a book that will change yours. This is that kind of book!

If you knew you were going to die, what would you do to stay alive? What if it was going to be painful, not only for you but for your loved ones? What if it was going to take a while, maybe years or decades? What would you be willing to do to stop it? What would you be willing to try? Guess what? We are ALL dying. Whether we are sick or as healthy as can be. All of us are dying, but very few of us are really living. Maybe life is going on all around you, years are passing, and you are going through the motions…but you're not really there. Or perhaps each day is filled with pain. Physical pain. Emotional Pain. Both.

For you, maybe "happiness" falls somewhere in the realm of unicorns and fairy tales. Something to be found in movies and storybooks but not in "real life." Or maybe happiness is real, only it's something that everyone else has…but something you cannot seem to find. If this is you, or someone you know…welcome. You will be entering familiar territory in these pages. But only for a while. Though I intend to share with you my personal experiences and challenges, the story takes a twist. For some, this twist will be too scary, too intimate, too costly to follow. Take heart, I was once there, also. Everyone needs to come in their own time, when the cost of staying becomes much higher than the cost of moving forward, into the unknown. For others, this twist will still be scary, painful, intimate…but something else too! Something incredible. Something that will forever change your perceptions of who you are. Of your past. Of your present. These few brave souls will find something that many only dream of…true freedom!

I don't know where this story finds you in your journey. But I do not think it is a coincidence that you are here. Thank you, brave soul, for showing up…no matter how long you stay!

WHO AM I?

I will begin this story in a rather odd place…THE END! See, I was dying. In December of 2011, I was at home, hooked up to an IV unit. I had been in the early stages of liver and kidney failure. My blood was "thick as molasses," I couldn't keep food down, and I was very sick. The list of diseases/ailments/conditions/syndromes that I had been diagnosed with was unbelievable. I mean truly, unbelievable. Had I not experienced every one of the appointments, blood tests, MRIs, tests, and scans and heard each diagnosis…I wouldn't believe it either. In fact, even though I had been to each of those…something inside of me still felt like "they've missed something." Something bigger, more foundational. How can one person have THIS MANY DISEASES??? Here is a list of some (not all) of the medically-diagnosed conditions I had acquired up to this point:

- Lyme Disease w/multiple co-infections (Babesia, Bartonella, etc.)
- Postural Orthostatic Tachycardia Syndrome (POTS)
- Cerebral Hyperfusion
- Dysbiosis
- Hashimoto's
- Graves' disease
- Goiter
- Adrenal Fatigue
- Celiac disease
- Migraines
- Thunderclap Headaches
- Candida
- Fibroids
- Endometriosis (2 surgeries)
- Infertility
- Ovarian Dysfunction
- Poor Uterine Blood Flow
- Fibromyalgia

Introduction

- Chronic Fatigue Syndrome
- Degenerative Disc Disease (surgery, epidural blocks, cortisone injections)
- Ankylosing Spondylitis
- Pilonidal Cyst/Abscess
- Plantar Fasciitis
- Nerve Damage
- Bone Spurs
- Crohn's Disease
- Spinal Meningitis
- Rheumatoid Arthritis (took injections & 2 orals)
- Reiter's Syndrome
- Hormone Imbalance
- Menorrhagia
- Polymicrobial State
- Intestinal Parasites (Trichinella, Plasmodium, Entamoeba Histolytica)
- Irritable Bowel Syndrome (IBS)
- High Risk for Pulmonary Embolism
- Depression
- and more…

The months leading up to December 2011 involved me going in twice a week for IV infusions, weekly blood draws, and a daily regimen of 180 medications/supplements/drops/injections A DAY. Yes, that is not a misprint. One hundred eighty medications either swallowed, injected, or administered. Every. Single. Day (no wonder I went into liver and kidney failure…RIGHT?). To be fair, this was not something that happened overnight. I will give you a little bit of my background.

I was never a "sickly" kid, but I wasn't exactly the picture of health. In my house growing up, it was totally normal to find multiple bottles of prescription medications in our cupboards. The majority of these were various kinds of antibiotics. I seemed to forever have strep throat, tonsillitis, flu, or some other random virus or bug. At the time, we didn't understand the dangers of overusing antibiotics and my mother believed she was being proactive (and financially wise) by giving us the antibiotics until we felt better, and then save the rest for the next time we got sick, which was often.

Still, I was a very active child. I rode horses, played sports, and never felt any different from any other kids (as far as physical health was concerned). Granted, I broke a lot of bones. I had measles, intestinal infections, a ruptured appendix, and a few other "uncommon" ailments. I developed migraines around 14 years old and began a prescription medication to try and manage them. I was also diagnosed with a "chemical imbalance" around 16. Labels like "bipolar" and "manic" were thrown around a bit, but I started medicating for that as well. This wasn't too concerning to me at the time. My entire family was on some sort of antidepressant and would often swap medications (more on that fun dynamic later).

See, we were of a fairly common belief that doctors were almost god-like individuals and that nearly every discomfort or dis-ease could be handled with a pill. I mean, if a doctor said it…it HAD to be "gospel." It was unheard of in my family to not be taking something. My family sort of threw around diagnoses like it was a game. A bit of a twisted game. Like being the "sickest" or worst off was the big winner! Of course, I wasn't consciously aware of this dynamic until I was much older. But I have digressed into the "Beginning"…I was starting at the End! More on that later!

My books, website, and profession are now called MIND CHANGE. The reason for this is simple. Though I have had countless inspirations, challenges, and changes in my 42 years of living…what is in this book is so radical, so different, it was like I had a brain transplant. Things that were intrinsically ME, became NOT ME any longer. What is the relevance of this for you? If you are unhappy with ANY part of your life, if you are finding yourself in the "same old patterns"—depression, dis-ease, addiction, illness, pain, mental conditions, worry, stress, anxiety or recurring "issues" with other people…this book can help you. In fact, if you are not living the life of your dreams…this book can help you.

We all come into this world with different environments, different parents, different DNA. We each face unique challenges and situations. And yet one thing is the same no matter who you are and where you come from…we can't choose our circumstances, but we CAN CHANGE the way we respond to them. We have a choice. We *each* have a choice. Some call it "free-will." But whatever you call it, it comes down to us. We get to choose. Choose life…Life to the full! My intention with this book is to help you do just that. Thank you for joining me on this journey. See you on the other side! I want to give this information to you. I want you to give it to someone you love. It's time to change the world…one mind at a time!

The Science Behind It All

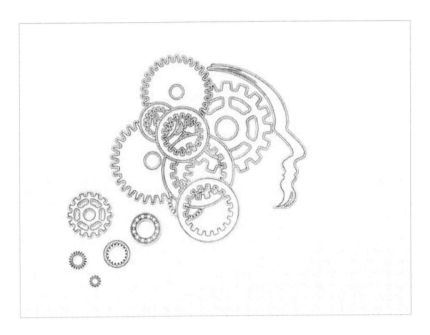

CHAPTER 1

Our Beautiful Brain

Considering the fact that your brain is solely responsible for you being able to even read this information and understand it, we are shockingly unacquainted with how it works. So, let me do a cursory introduction. Your brain is an incredibly complex and wonderful thing. It is THE most vital organ in your body. When the brain is at work, doing what it was created to do, we call that "the mind." In 2014, the New York Times called the "Human Brain" the next frontier in science. Paradoxically, it seems that the more we learn about our brains, the less we seem to know! For instance, it is still a widely held belief that we only use about 10% of our brain. That is categorically untrue. Science shows that we do, in fact, use the majority of our brain...though brain function still remains quite a mystery [1]. Even just 15 years ago, scientists believed that brain development peaked in the first few years of life. It is true that critical brain changes in the prefrontal cortex and limbic systems (areas involved in social decision-making, impulse control and emotional processing) happen primarily in adolescence. But our brain actually continues developing throughout our lives.

It wasn't until the 1960s that research began to suggest that the brain might not be as "hard-wired" as we once believed. Formerly, we thought the DNA with which we arrived would predict the ultimate (unavoidable) outcome of our lives. This meant that we would spend the first part of our lives learning from our parents, and the second half of our lives trying desperately NOT to end up like them! Only to wake up one day, look in the mirror, and realize that your mother is staring right back at you. Yes, yes...we are all familiar with the age-old "Nature vs. Nurture" debate that still has some folks tied up in knots. But over the last 20+ years, science has come to realize that those former beliefs were wrong. We are not hard-wired, at least not entirely. Let me explain.

When you were in utero, as a fetus, you began to "download" some of your basic operating systems, and in doing so, your brain began to grow. Where did that information come from? Yes, your DNA. From your parents, but also from the hundreds of thousands of years of brain evolution in humankind. Barring any genetic or environmental disruptions, you were born with some fundamental abilities that were "hard-wired" into your brain. Breathing, for instance. In the time that you took to read these first few paragraphs, you took an average of 6 breaths. Did you think about it? Nope! Breathing, thank goodness, is a skill with which you are very familiar with. In fact, you got a jump-start on that skill with some of your initial programming. With me so far?

While these seemingly "hard-wired" programs of breathing, digesting, cell production, and many other vital operations are essential (and thankfully automatic for most of us), even they are not fixed and permanent. Have you ever gone swimming? If so, you have likely held your breath for an extended period of time. If you are a good swimmer or swim at a competition level, you have fundamentally changed a skill that seemed to be hard-wired. You now possess the skill to override and control your breathing system. Many people have mastered the art of lowering their blood pressure by simply bringing awareness to their breath. Wow! We can literally change the rate at which our heart pumps blood through our bodies. And this is with basic operating systems for our survival! What does this mean for you?

We now know that the brain is actually "plastic." If you are like me, you may have just envisioned a Fisher-Price model of the brain inside your head. All color-coded and labeled in an array of pastel colors, unbending even to a toddler's determined hands! But rather than the stiff, cheap plastic we have become accustomed to in our children's toys, scientists use this term to refer to the brain's malleability. Neuroplasticity, or brain plasticity, refers to the brain's ability to CHANGE throughout life.

We've talked about the brain, and you now know that the mind is the brain at work. To handle an absolutely incredible task of being your brain, it splits the load. Dr. Joe Dispenza (best selling author and neuroscience researcher) breaks the brain down into 3 parts: the Thinking Brain, the Emotional Brain, and the Reptilian Brain.

THE TRIUNE BRAIN

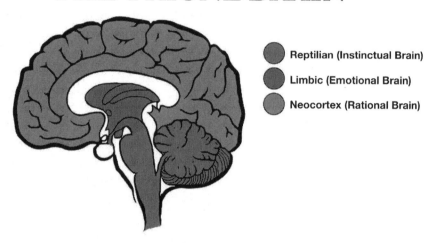

- Reptilian (Instinctual Brain)
- Limbic (Emotional Brain)
- Neocortex (Rational Brain)

The thinking brain is the Neo-Cortex, the most evolved part of the human brain. This is the place that forms new neurons with every new thought. In fact, it's the part of your brain you are using right now! Hello Neo Cortex!

Next is the Limbic Brain. Also known as the Emotional Brain or the Mammalian Brain. This part of your brain produces and regulates chemicals responsible for our feelings and emotions. Finally, the Reptilian Brain is the area in which your Cerebellum lies. I often refer to this as the Primal Brain. For those of you who are not particularly fascinated by brain research or factoids, don't leave me just yet! Though I have been deep diving in the recent discoveries in Neuroscience, Epigenetics and

Psychoneuroimmunology that is not what this book is about. Think of this book as sort of the "Cliffs Notes" to your brain.

These 3 brains and their relevant counterparts: the hippocampus, amygdala, and cerebellum are critical to what makes you, you. But luckily, you don't need to go back to medical school to understand and harness their power! I will address some of the individual systems within the brain as we progress, but for now, I'm not as interested in the brain and its anatomy as in the working of it. Again, the mind. Let's further clarify this by breaking the mind down into 2 categories, or operating systems if you will—the conscious mind and the subconscious/unconscious mind.

CHAPTER 2

Our Subconscious Mind: Outsourcing Our Data Entry

For the purpose of explanation, I am going to simplify the complex workings of our minds into an analogy. This isn't a new comparison. For many years, scientists have been comparing our brain to a computer. But just like the incredible advances that we have seen in technology, our understanding of the brain and mind have also grown. For a moment, I want you to imagine the human brain like a computer. Personally, I prefer Mac over PC. Even if you are a diehard PC lover, stick with me for analogy's sake! First...a disclaimer: I am one of the least tech-savvy people I know. So for those of you who are very knowledgeable in this area, bear with my rudimentary comparisons!

My MacBook Air came to me, preprogrammed with certain operating systems. It was already "hard-wired" with specific programs. There are things it does by itself without my knowledge or effort. One thing it does is provide the ability to create file folders so that I can organize all of the extra stuff I put into it. Though my husband and I each have a Mac, and they are basically the same model, they have very unique content based on what we individually decided to add. For instance, my husband is an incredible creator and editor of videos. To fulfill this hobby, he decided to download Final Cut Pro, which is an advanced video editing software program. This program came with countless files full of data that, once downloaded, allowed his Mac to run this program and produce the software to create and edit videos. Our brain has a similar "filing system." Let's call this the Subconscious Mind.

Dr. Joseph Dispenza, D.C. author of *You Are the Placebo*, states that the brain processes 400 billion bits of information a second. Yep, 400 billion, with a B!!! It is generally accepted that the conscious mind can handle 7 bits of information (plus or minus 2). Our subconscious minds have to find a way of reducing MILLIONS and MILLIONS of sensory messages every second, down to a level where it can process the messages and make sense of them.

If your conscious mind had to deal with the absolute barrage of information that we take in every second...it would melt down! So the subconscious mind comes to the rescue. Your internal programmer, the subconscious mind, filters through all of this information and decides what's important and then files this information into the proper files. So your brain is filled with all of these "file folders" that are chock full of information that you have been collecting since birth! Incredible, huh? If we were to do an MRI of your brain, these "folders" would show up as bright little clusters (see attached image). These are your neurons! And they are all connected to form a neuro-net highway in your brain. This conglomeration of bright little clusters holds the data that makes you who you are!

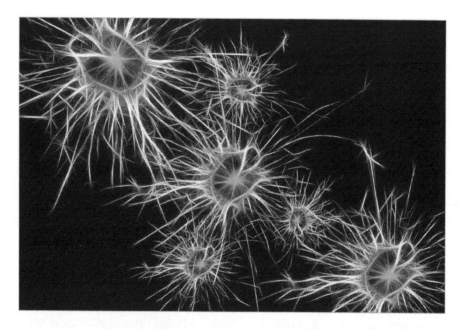

To illustrate this further, I would like to give you an example. Assuming you are over the age of 18 and one of the 87% of the population who can legally operate a motor vehicle, you have a skill we call driving. At what age did you learn to drive? Likely, the answer you provided to this question would hover somewhere around ages 14-16. What if I told you you were wrong? That you actually started to learn to drive the very first time you were cognitively aware of a car. Otherwise, driver's education would have been a MUCH longer course! How did you know how to get in the car? Which seat did you sit in to drive? How did you know what the steering wheel was used for? All of this knowledge that you have been accumulating concerning driving has been stored in a "file," or neuro cluster, in your brain. The nanosecond that your brain receives the message that you are going to need the relevant information, it pulls up the associated "file" and begins to produce the "skill" associated with this event. Though you are not consciously aware of it, your subconscious mind has sorted through the file and will now send the messages to the body to "do driving." You don't even have to think about it. And at this point, this skill is so rehearsed, so often utilized and practiced, that it becomes second nature. Haven't you ever arrived at work or the store and realized you don't even remember driving there? Yes? Now let's continue with this example to show how whatever data that file folder holds will be the outcome of how we operate.

Let's say that in your particular "file" labeled "driving," your mind finds a few negative resources. For instance, when you were 16, you and a few friends were messing around and took a corner on a dirt road a little too fast, and your car flipped over. Then, at 19, you were involved in a traffic accident that resulted in a fracture to your leg. And tragically, when you were in college, a group of friends who you were supposed to be riding with was involved in a head-on collision and one of your friends was killed. Let me ask you, do you think that you might have a different reaction to getting behind the wheel than someone who hadn't had these experiences?

Your subconscious mind has one primary objective when sorting through the millions and millions of bits of sensory input on a daily basis...to keep you safe. That's it. That is why it regulates your breathing, blood flow, digestion, and many other primal features to keep you alive daily. For this reason, Robert Smith, creator of FasterEFT, calls the subconscious mind the Intelligent Idiot. Intelligent because the subconscious mind is intelligent enough to process the billion bits of information you encounter daily and file it into the relevant categories to provide you with the needed skills for survival, but its "idiot" feature is that it does not judge these inputs the way the conscious mind does. The subconscious mind does not distinguish the difference between the danger of meeting a bear in the woods or getting up in front of a group of strangers to do a speech. It only recognizes something as "dangerous" if we have prior knowledge that it is. Most of us know from movies or stories that bears are not good company alone in the woods, but some people have equally terrifying experiences in front of crowds. Though consciously we would deem the bear encounter more dangerous, the subconscious mind might disagree, having far more references regarding the fears and dangers of public speaking.

So, back to the driving example. The person with the numerous references that driving is a potentially lethal activity will produce some things differently than the person without those same experiences. Let's say it's Susie that has the negative experiences that I referenced before, and Lisa does not. When Lisa gets behind the wheel to drive to work, her "file" is pulled up, and she automatically produces the skill of driving, and she can go about her driving normally. When Susie gets behind the wheel, a whole different outcome occurs. Susie's subconscious mind pulls up this file and notices that the file has been flagged. Because of her previous adverse experiences, her subconscious mind "flagged" this file as a potential threat or danger. In doing so, it needs to get the conscious mind's attention so that every system is on high alert for possible danger.

The subconscious mind and the conscious mind do not speak the same language. It's a good thing they don't. This is why. Our conscious mind is ever-changing depending on our moods, environments, and feelings. It's the language of emotions, feelings, and awareness. It's a fickle thing. If our conscious mind was responsible for our breathing, let's say, most of us would forget to breathe within the first minute! Our conscious mind is much more creative and whimsy, though it's responsible for creating what we call "our reality." If we feel it, it's real. If we think it, it must be right. If we see it, it's absolute. And seemingly, it has control during our waking hours.

Our subconscious mind is much more data-focused and logical. When we sleep, it does the majority of its sorting and filing from the data we received during the day. A good reason to get a good night's sleep! It doesn't spend time "feeling," it simply files. When it recognizes that an event from our day resulted in a negative reaction, it "flags" this memory and keeps an eye out for similar circumstances that might cause discomfort. The "flagging" process is actually the work of a little gland in the lower part of our brain called the Amygdala gland. Its basic function is to regulate our Fight, Flight, or Freeze response. If at any time during our day, we feel that we may be in danger, that little gland kicks in to assist in the solution. The subconscious mind makes a note of these particular events as "potentially dangerous," and it remains there unless another similar event comes through with a similar or elevated response, at which time, the subconscious mind files this as "known to be dangerous."

I am acutely aware of how I overly simplified some very complex systems. Though these individual systems and the way they function independently and together are fascinating, that information would take up numerous books. My purpose is to show you the results of this process and how it relates to changing our minds and, therefore, our lives. To give another illustration, I will provide you with an example of how an individual could develop a common but crippling phobia...fear of public speaking.

Justin, a well-kept man in his late 20s, walks into my office with quite a problem. Since before he can remember, he has been terrified of getting up in front of a crowd to speak. Though he cannot remember when it started, he feels that it has become worse the older he gets. Justin is up for a promotion at work that will involve presenting his team's ideas to upper management. Though he is very qualified, he has turned down the promotion in the past due to his fear of speaking publicly. He is now faced with a decision to stay in his current role and watch younger colleagues pass him by, or to take advantage of the higher salary and further promotions in his career. Not only is his professional life affected, but his personal life is on hold as well. At his current rate of pay, he isn't able to save enough money to buy an engagement ring he has wanted and has put off proposing to the girl of his dreams for much longer than anticipated. Yep, quite a predicament!

To pull all of our previously-mentioned information together in a practical example, let's look into Justin's mind, shall we? First, let's pull up the little neurocluster tucked nicely into his Hippocampus that is labeled "Public Speaking." This file is populated with every experience that he has personally experienced, heard about, saw, or watched on TV. The key is to travel back to the first known adverse experience that was "flagged" in this file. We find the jackpot! Something we call the Primary Imprint. This is the first known adverse experience we find within the file. As a side note, Justin is entirely oblivious to this particular memory. It has been stored in his subconscious mind and replayed countless times. But his conscious mind has remained unaware of it. Here is what this particular folder in the file contains: Kindergarten Show and Tell.

In kindergarten, Justin is a well-liked and well-adjusted boy. He feels comfortable and safe with his teacher and classmates. On this particular Friday, they have "Show and Tell." Justin has been anticipating this all week and can't wait to introduce his classmates to his favorite stuffed animal, Teddy. As Justin approaches the front of the class, he very much hopes they will like Teddy, too. Justin stands in front of the teacher's desk at the front of the room. He begins to tell the class about Teddy and how they came to be friends. In the middle of his explanation, the entire class suddenly bursts into raucous laughter. Justin stands in horror as the class laughs at him. He is mortified. Not only do they not like Teddy, but they also do not like him! Justin thought these were his friends. Now Billy is laughing so hard that he has fallen out of his chair. Justin's face flushes red, and he bursts into tears, running out of the room.

The brain is receiving all of this information and finds the appropriate response. It creates feelings of shame, embarrassment, hurt, and even anger. Because of the intense emotions being created, the Amygdala gland has been activated and made the decision that Justin should run to avoid any further harm. To prevent any possible recurrence of this awful event, the Amygdala gland "flags" this memory by attaching undesirable physiological responses to it. Now, anytime that the subconscious mind opens this folder and replays the memory, the body will produce the attached physiological responses as well.

Justin now has a "proof" or a "reference" in his file that public speaking can be a dangerous and painful event. Just one or two adverse experiences in a file full of good experiences usually will not result in an adverse reaction. But if enough folders contain these negative associations, the subconscious mind will automatically produce a behavior in alignment with the negative. But guess what? What if what happened to Justin wasn't the whole story? As Justin was facing the class, he is observing them through only one perspective. What he sees. In reality, as Justin was talking, his teacher was attempting to take her seat at her desk behind the place where Justin was speaking. Because it's a rolling chair, and Mrs. Brown was distracted by Justin's story, she completely missed her chair and fell flat on the ground! So, what were the kids really laughing at? Mrs. Brown!

But do you think Justin knew that? Nope. Even after it was explained to Justin, his memory (file folder) still shows the class laughing at him.

Mind Change

Though the explanation of what really happened made Justin consciously feel a little better, his subconscious mind still holds the memory and the attached responses the same way he saw it.

So guess what happens in 3rd grade when Justin has to get up in front of the class to give a book report? He has no conscious memory of the kindergarten event. But remember, **everything we do is a skill**. So when Justin's mind scans his folders for the skills he needs for this particular task, his mind pulls up (subconsciously) the kindergarten event, and for reasons he cannot explain, he begins to feel nervous. He knows the book and wrote a good report. He feels comfortable with his friends and teachers and has no reason he can (consciously) think of that he would be nervous, but he is. Thanks to the activation of the Amygdala gland, the body goes into a survival state. Granted, it's a low-grade danger. But the mind still warns the body by elevating the senses to have a heightened awareness of danger. For Justin, his body is on alert. Pulse raised, palms sweating, heart racing. Primally, he is ready for possible danger, which actually makes him more susceptible to finding it!

As he gets up to do his book report, he finds that it's easier to keep his eyes glued to the paper and not look up. His body, unbeknownst to him, is ready to catch even the slightest form of danger. At the back of the class, Angie passes a private note to Susie but Bobby intercepts it. As Bobby teases the horrified Angie with revealing the content of the note, the last few rows break out into laughter. Immediately, Justin reacts! "They are laughing at me!" his mind screams. And the flood of current emotions mixes with the emotions from the previous event. Justin is shattered.

Now, as his subconscious mind goes to file this information, it has a stronger "flag" for the situation. Each time that Justin is required to speak in front of others, he is prepared for the worst. By the time he has to present his final paper his senior year, Justin is nearly paralyzed with anxiety. This is a bold attempt by his subconscious mind to protect him. The level of danger is now at high alert, and the result is the mind communicating very strongly to the body. Along with the anxiety, Justin experiences an increased heart rate, lightheadedness, sweaty palms, and now he is extremely nauseous. This is the body's way of communicating what the subconscious mind is saying. THIS IS DANGEROUS!! With the final paper being half his grade, Justin tries to push through the physical warnings only to vomit on the entire first row and then pass out.

Now, Justin is sitting in my office with a full-blown case of Glossophobia, or fear of public speaking. I will say it again: Our behavior in any given situation is simply the output of data that was previously "uploaded" to our drive. If there are more adverse experiences (sad faces) found in the file folder in comparison to the positive experiences (happy faces), what do you think the outcome will be?

So is Justin a failure? NO! He is successfully producing this outcome. In fact, every time he goes to speak, he successfully produces the skill of Glossophobia. He doesn't have Glossophobia, he does it. Every time. Without fail. Good job, Justin! The problem is, Justin wants to be successful at something different. Right now, he has a well-practiced skill that produces a public speaking phobia, but he wants to be successful at getting up in front of people without the fear of passing out or vomiting on his audience!

I'm going to say something now that CANNOT be understated. Listening? Good, here goes. We will always produce from what we hold within. Did you catch that? Let me say it another way. An orange tree cannot produce apples. Not even if it really really wants to. As much as Justin would like to effortlessly stand in front of his peers and give a presentation, his mind/body literally won't let him. It's too dangerous.

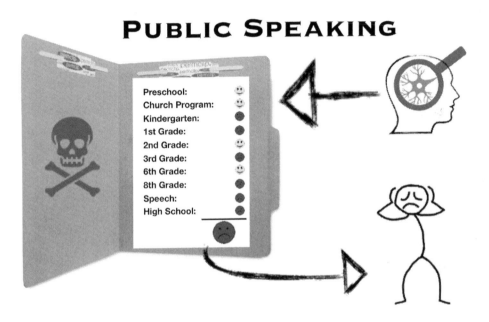

How do we apply this to our lives? Well, if we become aware that everything we think or do is actually a skill, then it should change our perception of everything.

Remember, our brain is the wheelhouse for our entire body. The body cannot do anything without the approval of the brain. This leads us to an essential understanding that I will repeat again.

Everything We Do Is A Skill

Human beings are learning machines!! From the moment we are born (and even before that) we are gaining skills. Some of those skills are a little more basic and are starting to be practiced even in the womb. Breathing, eating, hearing…these skills (though done differently inside the womb) are being developed even prior to being born. The "skill" of eating, which we all possess and use regularly, has had quite an evolution! After birth, the skill that we had been developing and practicing in the womb (sucking/digesting/etc.) now faces a new learning. Depending on whether you are breastfed or bottle-fed, each child needs to add new layers to the "skill" of eating. As we get older, depending on our influences and environment, our skills will develop and change until it becomes second nature and we don't have to think about it at all (at least consciously)!

Remember the computer analogy? We need to be programmed, all of us. The majority of us come with the basic, similar hardware when we enter the world. But after that, our "programming" is highly subjective, given our environment and upbringing. For instance, with the eating example, if you were brought up in China, you may have learned to eat with chopsticks rather than a fork or spoon. This will become second-nature to you. Later, as you encounter more Western influences, you may have to become accustomed to using unfamiliar tools. We are ALL programmed. We have to be. Everything we do, from driving a car to walking to how to cope with stress, is a learned behavior.

There are about 100 billion neurons (folders in the files) in a human brain, which is about the same as the number of stars in the Milky Way galaxy. Our unconscious mind has a bunch of filters that delete, distort, and generalize external events that we see, hear, feel, or read about. These filters have been programmed by our experiences in life and thus distort, delete, and generalize around according to our previous programming. This is what we refer to as "our reality." The interesting part of this equation that equals "reality" is that it comes from our own personal programming. Which makes it subjective! This is SO huge. We can argue it all we want, but research shows that what we think is "real" is only an outward projection of what we hold within [1]. Each of us is unique with regard to what we hold. This leads us back to the issue of "problems." To understand WHY we have problems, we need to look again at how we create our problems. For another illustration, I would like to share a story from Gilda Radner's book, *It's Always Something*:

"When I was little, Dibby told me a story about her cousin who had a dog— just a mutt—and the dog was pregnant. I don't know how long dogs are pregnant, but she was due to have her puppies in about a week. She was out in the yard one day and got in the way of the lawnmower and her two back legs got cut off. They rushed her to the vet who said, 'I can sew her up, or you can put her to sleep if you want. But the puppies are OK—she'll be able to deliver the puppies.' Dibby's cousin said, 'keep her alive.' So the vet sewed up her backside and over the next week that dog learned how to walk. She didn't spend any time worrying; she just learned to walk by taking two steps in the front and flipping up her backside and then taking two more steps and flipping up her

backside again. She gave birth to six little puppies, all in perfect health. She nursed them and then weaned them. And when they learned to walk, they all walked like her." (Radner, 1989)

"They all walked like her."…powerful illustration, right? You see, the puppies had perfectly functioning back legs, but because of their earliest "programming," they didn't use those legs as they were intended. As those puppies grow and begin to interact with other dogs, we see a number of different scenarios. Let's say that half of the puppies decide that they can get around much more quickly if they actually use those back legs. They have places to go and shoes to chew up! Their little brains scan all of the available files to make sure this is not a "dangerous" option, and if no "flags" are found, this becomes a possibility. So by choosing this option, they use their mind to tell their brain, "Hey, we would actually like to use these other two legs as well." The brain responds by telling the body to increase blood flow to the back legs and with a little practice, Voilà, the puppies are walking normally. The other half of the litter decides that they don't really need the back legs. "Mom seems to manage fine, those tall human folks seem to always bring the food to us and even pick us up and carry us when we need." For these puppies, the mind communicates to the brain that the back legs are not needed and the brain responds by reducing blood flow. This leads to muscle atrophy and eventual paralysis of the back legs. The brain (computer) is able to run either program, "need back legs" or "don't need back legs." The mind needs to decide which. To do so, it performs a basic cost/benefit analysis to see which decision has the biggest "payoff" and is the safest option.

Again, this will be different for each puppy, depending on how they process the world. So if our brains work perfectly, and we are not actually "broken," why do we have problems? I'm so glad you asked!

Let's Just Blame It On Our Parents

As easy as it would seem to just blame all of our problems on our parents or our upbringing, it's not that simple. You have seen proof. Multiple children grow up in the same abusive and alcoholic home. One grows up to be seemingly well adjusted, and the other becomes an addict. I want to show you that our upbringing and surroundings as a child have an undeniable effect on how we process the world, but we cannot necessarily *blame* those circumstances for our current behavior. In the next chapter, I'll explain why we aren't as "messed up" as we think we are.

CHAPTER 3

"Why Am I Such A Mess?"

"You are not responsible for the programming you picked up in childhood. However, as an adult, you are one hundred percent responsible for fixing it."

Ken Keyes Jr.

"Why am I such a mess?" "What is wrong with me?" These are questions I used to ask myself all the time. I could come up with countless answers:

- It's my parents' fault

- I come from a long line of messed up people
- We didn't have enough money and I didn't have access to the same opportunities/knowledge/support that other people did
- I have a genetic condition
- It's the generation I was born in
- I just make bad choices
- I wasn't pretty enough
- I wasn't talented enough
- and on, and on, and on…

Do any of these sound familiar to you? I don't ask myself this question anymore! Neuro-linguistic Programming (NLP) teaches that we all operate from our own unique Model of the World.

NLP Communication Model

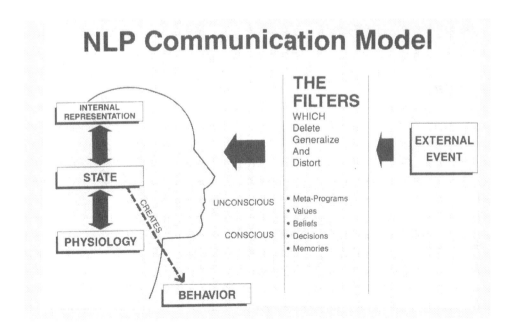

Bandler and Grinder explain it this way.

"No two human beings have exactly the same experiences. The model that we create to guide us in the world is based in part upon our experiences. Each of us may, then, create a different model of the world we share and thus come to live in a somewhat different reality..."
(Bandler & Grinder 1975: 7)

Basically, this explains that each of us operates from our own unique "Model of the World" or way of thinking. Let's take an example to illustrate this.

External Event: Child's Birthday Party

Observe the behavior of Parent A, who we will call Susan, and Parent B, who we will call Jane. Both have children who are attending the birthday party of a friend from kindergarten. Up to this point, both of these parents have been casually enjoying conversation with the other adults present. The mother of the birthday girl excitedly calls the party to attention to introduce the special guest who is about to arrive. Children and parents wait in expectation for the mystery guest. Soon, a large man dressed as a clown arrives and begins to engage the children with magic and balloon animals. Let's observe the reactions of these parents and, using the model above, try to guess the resulting behavior.

Susan: Susan is presented with the "External Event" of the clown arriving. Within seconds, her subconscious mind has analyzed all relevant data stored in the mind with regard to clowns. She deletes, distorts, and generalizes the countless bits of information that are occurring so that she can decide a course of action (behavior). In her mind, she is brought back to her own childhood and visiting the circus with her beloved grandparents. The smell of popcorn, peanuts, and cotton candy flood her mind and she can almost taste the candy apple. She sees all the bright colors and remembers the excitement welling up in her as a small child as the clowns jumped around the ring. She can even feel her grandparents love as she hears the sounds of the circus all around her. Even as she stands here 20 years later, she can actually feel the same excitement. Her heart beats faster and she is filled with excitement that her daughter is about to share in this moment! She laughs out loud and begins to cheer the clown along. Smiling broadly, she looks at her own daughter, expecting the same excitement.

Jane: Jane is presented with the same "External Event." She too uses her subconscious mind to analyze all relevant data stored in the mind with regard to clowns. Consciously, she has no particular problem with clowns. Nonetheless, a bad feeling comes over her and her mood darkens. Inexplicably, she is taken back to a childhood memory of being in the hospital and waking up in pain. She vaguely remembers the accident during a parade in her hometown. One minute she is watching in awe as the floats are passing in front of her throwing candy to all the children, and the next thing she knows, she wakes up in the hospital. The subconscious mind has accessed this memory for one very important detail. As she ran out into the street to grab the candy, she was hit by an oncoming vehicle. Though consciously she never was aware of it, the first person to reach her before she blacked out was one of the clowns in the parade.

Subconsciously, in her little mind, the connection was made. Clowns equal pain and fear. Though she does not consciously "remember" this detail, the subconscious mind does and deems it relevant information to the current external event. Within seconds, Jane is not feeling very well and is compelled to grab her daughter and remove her from the party. As the confused child protests, Jane explains that she suddenly does not feel well and they need to leave. "Besides, clowns are scary anyway!"

So, which scenario is reality? Who is right? Is the clown dangerous and scary, or a joyful opportunity? I know, I know…there are many people who are cheering for Jane right now because YOU don't like clowns! Have you ever considered why? Why does a clown bring joy to some and strike fear in the hearts of others? I don't know how I felt about clowns prior to the age of 10, but thanks to watching Poltergeist when I was 10 and reading Stephen King's IT a couple years later…I have never viewed clowns the same! Welcome to how you develop your Model of the World!

Why We Do What We Do

Remember above when I mentioned that I don't ask, "Why am I so messed up?" anymore? Well, this is why. Something can only be "messed up" or broken when it OUTPUTS something different than what was INPUT. Bear with me! If you put your pizza in the microwave to reheat it, you expect to open the microwave and find…pizza! Right? Maybe a little warmer than you left it…but pizza nonetheless. If you put in pizza and got out apple pie, you might be happy at first, but your microwave would be "messed up" or "broken." I am lucky enough to live on Maui in Hawaii. We have multiple fruit trees in our backyard. It would be very odd if my mango tree suddenly started producing avocados. I'm going to say it again...

You can only produce what you hold within.

This knowledge (along with applications that you will find later in this book) means more fulfillment in life is achievable when we are less affected by external circumstances, through gaining control of our internal processes. This leads to mental freedom, empowered responses, and mindful interactions with others. This is where to start:

Two Models Of Thinking: Victim Or Victor

From the moment we are born, we begin building our unique and individual Model of the World. As human beings, we are born almost entirely helpless. We are totally dependent on the care of others to be alive. That sets the stage for a very "dependent driven" model of the world. This serves a baby and child well. Our brains are a virtual blank slate and we need to learn EVERYTHING. We need to learn to walk, talk, feed ourselves, go to the bathroom...everything. Though we are incredibly complex as humans, we are born with very few survival skills and mechanisms. Depending on our experiences, each child will develop their own Model of the World. This early development is very cause/

effect oriented. "I cry, I get food." "I soil myself, someone changes me." Also, notice that it is very "self-focused" as well. There is no thought in a baby's brain for the mother. "Wow, Mom! I can see that you have had no sleep since I came around. Why don't you go take a break? I'll just entertain myself for a bit." Don't we all wish!

Basically, because we do require another human being to provide for our very survival when we are young, we are almost always the "victim" of anything that doesn't go our way. As an example, if a baby is born to a mother addicted to methamphetamines, we simply cannot ascribe fault to that baby if it dies of starvation or neglect. It couldn't get away, reason with the mother, call for help or feed itself. This infant would unequivocally be a "victim." I think we can all agree on that. This "dependent driven" model of thinking lasts into our late adolescent to early teen years. The problem is that a good percentage of the population never graduates out of this model of thinking. What we see is an unwillingness to mature at the most basic of levels.

Robert Smith, the creator of FasterEFT/Eutaptics, calls the models of thinking "the lower" and "the upper" models of thinking. Though other versions of these models of thinking exist, I have chosen to narrow it down to two primary mindsets and call them the "Victim" and the "Victor." Before I get into the "nuts and bolts" of these models of thinking, we need to address the word "victim."

Victim...A 4-Letter Word?

The word victim has an interesting beginning. The root *vict* comes from Latin where it has the meaning "conquer." The words victor and victim come from the same origin—victor meaning the conqueror and victim being the one conquered. First recorded in 1490–1500, we see the Latin word *victima*, which described a sacrificial animal. This noun is now defined in the Random House Unabridged Dictionary as:

1. a person who suffers from a destructive or injurious action or agency: a victim of an automobile accident.

2. a person who is deceived or cheated, as by his or her own emotions or ignorance, by the dishonesty of others, or by some impersonal agency: a victim of misplaced confidence; the victim of a swindler; a victim of an optical illusion.

3. a person or animal sacrificed or regarded as sacrificed: war victims.

I have personally struggled with this word and "label." Having grown up in a home and family wrought with drug/alcohol addiction and sexual/physical abuse, I certainly felt like a victim growing up! I definitely relate to definition #2 from Random House. Deceived? Uh-huh. Cheated? Yup. I will go into more detail later about my personal story, but I can assure you that I felt like a victim more times than not. The problem was...I began to feel MORE and MORE victimized as I grew older. Though I was no longer in danger, abused, or neglected by members of my family, I still felt like I was being deceived/cheated/neglected in many areas of my life.

It is true, bad things happen. While we are alive on this planet, I don't foresee an end to that. There will always be perpetrators and there will always be victims of those perpetrations. So what is the difference between being a victim of a perpetration and having a victim mindset? I think a key to this lies in the second definition listed above. Notice #2, "a person who is deceived or cheated, as by his or her own emotions or ignorance...."

In my personal life and my field of work, it has become important to differentiate between being a victim of a perpetration and having a victim mindset. We need to be very careful not to "blame the victim." Two seemingly opposing articles from Psychology Today appear to capture the spirit of this debate. The first article, entitled *When Did "Victim" Become a Bad Word?: Why do we despise weakness in ourselves and others?* by Beverly Engel L.M.F.T., warns us of the dangers of "victim shaming."

"We are a culture of people who despise weakness when we see it. In that way we are all bullies to one degree or another. Think about it. Who are the school yard bullies? Research and experience have told us that bullies are children who have been abused themselves in their home or elsewhere. They are kids who are enraged because someone has been picking on them. And they are kids who feel humiliated and shamed because they have been victimized. So what do they do with their rage? They can't take it out on their abusers, who are usually adults or older children who

are much stronger or who have more power and authority than they do. So they take their rage out on those who are smaller and weaker than themselves. And what do they do with their overwhelming shame at having been overpowered? They punish those who remind them of their own weakness and vulnerability.

"It is no wonder that we are raising yet another generation of bullies and abusers. Unless we turn this thing around and make it OK to admit when we have been victimized, admit when we feel bad, and not allow other people to shame us for it, the cycle will continue.

"Not only do we ignore the cries of victims and thus miss the opportunity for us to reach out to them in compassion, but we end up blaming the victim. Because we can't tolerate weakness in others because it reminds us of our own weakness and vulnerability. We must find a way to protect ourselves from them. What better way to do this than to blame the victim for his or her own victimization? If the young woman who was raped at a college fraternity party hadn't been drunk, she wouldn't have been gang-raped. After all, she put herself in a dangerous situation. She should have known better. It's her own fault." [1]

The second article, entitled *Are You Ready to Stop Feeling Like a Victim?* by Nancy Colier LCSW, Rev., captures the essence of the "victim mindset":

"It's psychologically healthy to acknowledge the suffering and feelings of powerlessness that accompany such experiences. And yet, there are those people who feel like victims all the time, regardless of their circumstances. Those with a victim mentality are always being victimized, at least in their own mind. They maintain a consistent victim identity and see life through perpetually victim-tinted glasses."

"We all know people who seem to be constantly commenting on some injustice done to them — how others are denying them what they need, want, and deserve, controlling them against their will, and making them do what they don't want to do. Or how life is against them and the universe is designed to punish them, personally. Perhaps you yourself are someone who experiences life this way." [2]

We all know people like this, right? I believe I was one of them. For a long time. So where should we stand on this? Well, I think somewhere in the middle is a great start! I also believe that acknowledging the two models of mindset, Victim or Victor, will help us. Let's view these models in diagram form, and then we can move on to discuss it a bit further.

The Victim Model

This is the model of thinking with which we come into the world. See the child in the middle, literally a victim of the necessary influencers. Though many of these "outside forces" or "influencers" may vary per child, the principle remains the same. We are undeniably influenced by our caregivers (parents, grandparents, other family members). Contrary to some teachings and beliefs out there, I do not believe that we *choose* our family of origin before birth. If that were the case, we have a LOT of masochistic souls out there. Rather, I believe we cannot choose anything with regard to our birth or family of origin.

In Model 1, the Victim Model, you see that the individual is surrounded by, or trapped by, the world around them. The common mantra of someone in this Model of thinking is "THEY are doing it to me." Of course the "they" and the "it" can be any number of things and people.

"The FOOD is making me fat."

"My parents abandoned me, so I cannot trust people."

"My coworkers make me feel bad."

"I wouldn't get so angry if my husband would just listen to me."

"Nobody understands my situation."

"I'm depressed because nobody will love me."

"I can't do it because of my ADHD/CFS/Fibromyalgia/Depression/ (enter diagnosis)."

"My whole family loses their temper, we are just angry people."

"I carry the gene for addiction, so that is why I abuse alcohol."

"You shouldn't get your hopes up, someone will always let you down."

The list goes on. In many ways, we are taught to continue in this Model of thinking. Everywhere we look, people are searching for the reason that we are the way we are. Our society and culture promote the idea that we all need something or someone else to fulfill us. We have given the responsibility for our health and wellness to doctors, responsibility for our spirituality to churches and preachers, responsibility for our financial health to the government or economy, and so on. We feel helpless until "they" tell us what to do, believe, eat, wear. When it doesn't work out, we blame those that we gave that responsibility.

But it's not all bad! The Victim Model of thinking comes with perks. Being a victim gives you power. Power to avoid personal responsibility. This power allows you to feel "righteously" sad and persecuted, avoid uncomfortable emotions, and to manipulate other people. What people neglect to realize is that the "power" that they desperately seek is being handed over to others. This model of thinking puts the power of how to think/act/feel outside of themselves. Because they have relinquished any responsibility for self, they now must find their value in the opinion of others. The saddest part about this model of thinking is just how much time and energy is spent on continuing to feel this way. Though people get better and better at what they practice and the Victim Model comes naturally, these people are spending a tremendous amount of effort on feeling terrible!

Though our caregivers are likely our biggest influencers, other people or entities have a significant effect. Teachers, ministers, and friends are early influencers. TV, social media, politicians, doctors, and many other influences contribute to the way we shape and view our world.

DARLA & SHERRI

Let's take two examples of people who I have worked with. Sherri was raised in the Midwest in a devoutly Christian home. Sherri's parents were strict and dogmatic, but Sherri never doubted their love or approval.

Mind Change

Sherri's family shunned politics and media and allowed little contact with people they felt were "lost." Sherri sensed that childrearing was a harrowing experience and that sin and danger lurked around every corner. She felt oppressed at times and went through times of rebellion. Though her parents never forced her to follow their belief system and encouraged her to think for herself, Sherri sometimes felt responsible for keeping herself "in line." Despite this, Sherri believed she had a strong support system in her family and in her church and felt confident in her own identity.

Darla, on the other hand, was raised in a very "non-traditional" home. Darla's parents were lesbians. Both of her moms were liberal and very involved in activism and politics. While both moms claimed to be feminists, and they encouraged Darla to explore her own feelings and beliefs around being a woman. Darla often struggled with the "non-parental" role that her mothers' took. Essentially allowing Darla to make her own rules, they believed they were empowering Darla to be the "strong woman" she was intended to be. They did not believe in discipline and allowed Darla to simply learn her lessons from her mistakes. Although this approach was envied by many of Darla's friends, most of the time Darla wished she had a "normal" life and longed for structure.

Interestingly, both of these women came to me as clients, struggling with the exact same "problem." Both women were battling infertility. Though both women had grown up feeling loved and supported, their individual environments led to feelings of fear and inadequacy when it came to the role of "being a mother."

Infertility can often be a result of a subconscious fear or intimidation at the idea of being a parent. It can also signify deep unresolved issues with their own mother. Though not necessarily "traumatizing," a person who struggled with too many responsibilities as a child can have a deep fear that having a child will be overwhelming and may take up the little bit of free time or energy that they have. Again, these are usually deep-seated and subconscious programs. They were input as a child, through a child's understanding.

Both Darla and Sherri had "good" childhoods. Upon further inspection, however, both also had a good deal of unresolved anger with their mothers. This deep internal conflict kept their bodies from fulfilling a natural and desired outcome—pregnancy. In both women, we had to go back and deal with the "victimized" child within. Individually and through different approaches, both women perceived that motherhood was a difficult and fearsome task. For Sherri, this played out through control and fear-based parenting. For Darla, this manifested as "unparenting." Though they were both now adults, they were still manifesting their childhood confusion in their bodies. We eventually healed the inner relationship with their mothers and their childhoods and both women ended up conceiving and having an easy labor and delivery.

Neither one of these women would have said they felt like "victims," but they were operating from a belief that said otherwise. When they took back their power and realized that they had filtered much of what their parents had been trying to do, they found compassion and forgiveness. Through this, they took responsibility and made peace within. The feeling of empowerment was much more conducive to child-rearing than victimization.

The Victim Mindset says, "THEY are doing it to ME." Who is "they"? "They" is whoever is being held responsible for the discomfort. The problem actually is the way we perceive power.

The Problem With Power

The main problem with the Victim Mindset is where we place the power. In this mindset, the power is outside of us. We give "them" the power to "make us" feel or do something. But see, it's actually OUR power to give power. Does that make sense? No person, place, or thing can *make you* feel a certain way. Only YOU have the power to determine how you will react to the things that happen around you. We often think people are "taking away our power," and yes, when you were a child that was possible. But as adults, what we do in our minds is far more powerful than what someone is trying to do to us. Viktor E. Frankl, an Austrian neurologist and psychiatrist, as well as a Holocaust survivor said this: *"Everything can be taken from a man but one thing: the last of the human freedoms—to choose one's attitude in any given set of circumstances, to choose one's own way."* [3]

Unspeakable atrocities have been perpetrated upon countless individuals over the time of man. I am not, in any way, trying to minimize that. Being victimized is rarely our choice, *staying* a victim is. More on that later!

THE VICTIM MINDSET
The power is *outside of us*

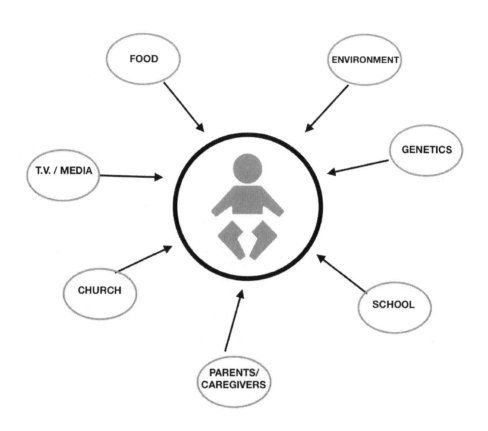

"**THEY**" are doing it to me

THE VICTOR MINDSET
The power is *inside of us*

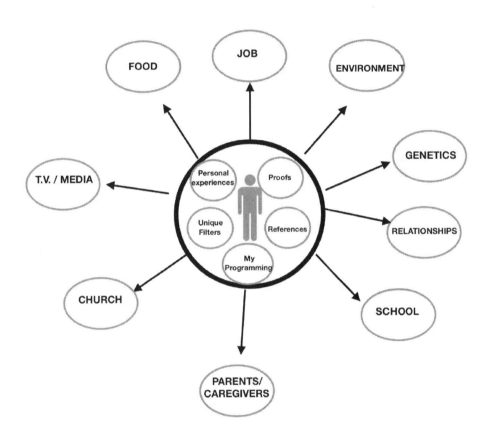

I take **COMPLETE RESPONSIBILITY** for my choices, actions, reactions, feelings and emotions.

The Victor Model

Look back at the diagram of the two models. We have established that the "lower model" is the Victim Model. So now, let's look at the Victor Model. The word "victor" comes from the Latin word meaning "to conquer." This is some of what Webster has to say [4]:

vic·tor

noun: victor; plural noun: victors

- a person who defeats an enemy or opponent in a battle, game, or other competition; "congratulations to the victors"

synonyms: winner, champion, conqueror, vanquisher, conquering hero, prize winner, medalist, cup winner, champ, top dog, number one

Remember I mentioned power? While the Victim Model puts the power *outside* of you, the Victor Model puts the power back where it really is...*within*. Living from this model of thinking shifts the power and responsibility back to you. Here we recognize that, though our family of origin and personal experiences in this world have shaped us, WE are in control over the way we feel about a situation and, as a result, the choices we make. Each one of us contains a unique set of experiences, filters, and perceptions. When we realize it is through *those* things that we evaluate the world around us, the power comes back to us.

Mind Change

We realize and understand that we are creators of the world around us. Though we cannot always control what people do around us or to us, we can have complete authority of the way we feel about it and what we do with it. Instead of giving others the power over how we feel, we take responsibility and realize the choice is ours. So rather than saying and believing, "You made me angry when you did that!," we can say, "I am angry about this." Even better, we don't have to *choose* to be angry, even if it's what we have always done in the past. If we feel angry, we realize it is our choice to be angry. This empowers us! If I chose to be angry, I can also choose to be something different instead. It doesn't mean that the situation didn't happen, it just means that you are taking control of the outcome.

Let's take traffic as an example. Likely, all of us are familiar with the unpleasant experience of being stuck in traffic or dealing with road rage. Say that you are driving to work one morning and somebody cuts you off. The Victim Model says, "I cannot believe that guy did that to me!" Because you now perceive that you were personally affected and targeted, you must retaliate. You may honk loudly and gesture wildly to convey the near-death experience that the person just caused. Or perhaps you yell loudly and proceed to give them a detailed account of what a terrible driver they are, of course, they can't hear you...but still! Or you could wait until the next light and strategically place yourself in the next lane so that you can turn slowly and give an epic "stink-eye." All of this, in response to "what *they* did to you." The Victor Model says, I can choose to be angry or I can choose to be at peace. If you typically choose the lower, victimized model, your first inclination will be to *do* anger. That is your "go-to" response. You likely practice this daily and therefore, are very good at it. BUT...when you recognize it's actually your *choice* how to feel and react, the power is back inside of you.

Dangers Of The Victor Model

Remember I said earlier that the Victor Model shifts the power and responsibility back to you? We like the idea of *power* being ours, but *responsibility*...not so much. I will be the first to admit that blame-shifting is MUCH easier than taking responsibility. At least at first glance. If *they* made me do it, then I am not technically responsible for my actions. Of course, this is almost never true. You know the old saying, *"With great power, comes great responsibility."* I would like to illustrate this with a case study of a client:

CHARLIE:

A man named Charlie* came to me with a problem with his right hip. He was using a cane and was very obviously in discomfort. I know that hip problems are generally related to a fear of moving forward due to a lack of trust or confidence in one's self. This is almost always associated with a "power struggle" in the home of origin. This usually plays out as domination of the child through demoralization or suppression.

I quickly inquired about his family of origin and the relationship with his mother and father. I was especially interested in the father relationship, given the right hip was involved. Charlie soon described a home filled with numerous children and a mother who was incredibly insecure and manipulative. Charlie spoke with venom as he described her constant desire to put the children down and mock their failures. When I inquired about the father, Charlie said he believed that his father was more interested in keeping himself in the mother's "good graces" and out of the line of fire. As a young man, Charlie made attempts to earn his mother's and father's love by being the best he could be at whatever he did. But those accomplishments only brought more criticism from his mother. I remember Charlie describing his father as "crippled" when it came to standing up to his mother.

Not surprisingly, Charlie went on to be very successful in his career and field of work. The skills he learned in the home, being the best he could be at what he did, were useful in the cutthroat corporate world. Also not surprisingly, in nearly every company he worked for, he would have a supervisor who would undermine his work and accomplishments. Just when it seemed that Charlie was going to "make it big," something would sabotage his progress, and he would need to start all over from the bottom. He felt victimized by upper management. In his personal life, the women he attracted were manipulative and abusive. Over and over, Charlie found himself in a battle to be respected and heard. It was showing up in every area of his life.

In our sessions together, we mended the relationship with his father and mother (both of whom had passed many years earlier). When I helped Charlie see that he had the power to view these relationships from a higher perspective, he finally gave himself the respect and love that he had always been chasing, and it began to show up in his present life. Charlie held much resentment and anger toward his caregivers, especially his mother, ultimately blaming her for his lack of success. But within a short time, he began to realize how hurt and alone she had felt for all those years. Charlie began to go back in his mind and give his mother the love that she had clearly been missing. As he did that, he was finally able to accept the love that his mother had been able to show for all those years. Subsequently, his hip pain completely disappeared. As a side effect, his relationships with his siblings dramatically improved, and he began to build a business for himself teaching others to be successful in their careers!

CHAPTER 4

Thoughts = Things

Now that you have been forever enlightened regarding your power, what are you going to do with it? Hopefully, you will begin to "try out" this newfound power and begin to see everything differently. And from this new perspective, begin to create the life of your dreams! But just in case you are not completely convinced, I should probably let you know that you are already creating. In fact, we are creating our world daily and then *perceiving* it as our reality. Let me explain.

Thoughts = Things

Have you ever felt controlled by a thought? You can be going along, minding your own business, and then a random but powerful thought enters your mind and takes over. "I wonder if my coworker is mad at me." You weren't even thinking about work, but now, this seemingly random thought enters your mind, and you can't shake it. You were just driving home, listening to the radio and thinking of what you were going to make for dinner. Now, you are engaged in a full-on mental investigation into your day to see if you can figure out why your coworker may have been mad at you. "Did I say something that offended her?" You rack your brain and replay the conversations from earlier in the day to see where the possible offense may have been. "Maybe someone told her I said something about her." Now, you are going through a list of possible suspects in your mind. If someone were to be a casual observer of your mind and body, they would notice that your mood and body language dramatically changed, even though the outside environment remained the same.

See, thoughts are things. Actual things. In a minute, we will look at the chemical make-up of a thought. But for now, just know that thought produces feelings and emotions, and those feelings and emotions create our mood and perceived reality. When we think, the physical nature of our brain changes. Prentice Mulford, who wrote *Thoughts Are Things* in 1889, states that "we think in matter," meaning that when we produce a thought, matter is produced. Even Sigmund Freud speculated in the early 1800s that our thoughts could change our brain.

Toxic Thoughts

Interestingly enough, a toxic thought and a healthy thought can be recognized under magnification! In Dr. Caroline Leaf's book, *Switch on Your Brain,* she shows an adapted graphic sketch of a Healthy Thought vs. a Toxic Thought. [1]

NEUROPLASTICITY:
The brain is malleable like plastic and can be changed moment-by-moment by how we direct our thinking

THE TOXIC THOUGHT   **THE HEALTHY THOUGHT**

Images from *Switch On Your Brain* by Dr. Caroline Leaf

It's at this point I would love to completely "geek out" and go into all of the science behind the molecular makeup of a thought and how it literally *changes* the landscape of our brain. But far brighter and more studied individuals have made this knowledge their life's work, and I have at least 5-6 books on my desk currently that focus solely on this research (don't worry, for fellow research geeks, I have included a substantial reading list at the end of this book). For the sake of time and our collective sanity, I will ask that you accept my humble "layman's" version of these truths.

Emotions Aren't Real

At least not in the way you probably think. The classical view of emotions is that emotions are things that happen *to you*. We are taught, incorrectly, that emotions are hardwired "feelings" that we should control, suppress, accept, or release. For example, someone or something "triggers" an emotion and a stress response ("fight-flight-freeze") in us, and we can use mindfulness to notice, acknowledge, and "release" this emotion. This still implies that something outside of us is causing something *inside* of us (Victim Model).

When you think a thought, you have just created matter. In order to figure out what to do with this newly created matter, the brain must make meaning of this sensory input to prepare for what the body needs to do next. As you now know, the way it does this is by scanning all of our internal files to find the closest previous experience to relate to. The brain prepares the body to respond physiologically (through our nervous, cardiovascular, immune, endocrine, and musculoskeletal systems). Emotions are the *nearly instantaneous* meanings the brain gives to these external and internal sensory input (bodily sensations). Lisa Feldman Barrett, a neuroscientist at Northeastern University, and author of *How Emotions Are Made* puts it best [2]:

"In other words, emotions are your brain's best guess of how you should feel in the moment. Emotions aren't wired into your brain like little circuits; they're made on demand. As a result, you have more control over your emotions than you might think." (Barrett, 2017)

So emotions are our own personal creation! Taking the Victor mindset, that means if we acknowledge that it is our creation, we can also decide to create something different. This places responsibility right back where it belongs—inside of us. At this point, you may be feeling a little uncomfortable. We've spent the last decade or two trying to "get in touch" with our emotions, just to find out that they aren't even real!! The implications of understanding this perfectly-designed engineering achievement are huge! If we are actually the creators of our emotions, then it stands to reason that we could *create* an emotionally-fulfilling life.

Am I saying that emotions are useless or should be avoided? By no means! Emotions provide incredible insight into our internal wiring. Let me offer another practical example:

Event: A local networking dinner for professional women

Who: Darla and Wanda

Two different women of basically the same age, social status, and life stage. Darla and Wanda each choose to attend the event for similar reasons. Both desire to build their local networking portfolio and feel that this event could provide opportunities.

Darla arrives at the event and walks into the room, instantly noticing a large group of women gathered together in animated conversation.

Instantly, for no apparent reason, Darla is "triggered" and begins to feel insecure. She is sure that the women in the group took note of her arrival and have already judged her. In fact, she is nearly certain that they are indiscreetly taking turns looking at her and laughing. Darla instantly regrets this decision and hurries off to the ladies' room to decide whether this humiliation is going to be worth it. Shoulders slumped and eyes to the ground, she hopes nobody else is in the bathroom when she arrives. Later on, when she arrives back home, Darla cries to her husband about the awful experience. She should have known better...this kind of thing *always* happens to her!

Wanda arrives at the same event just after Darla leaves for the ladies' room. As Wanda enters the room, she sees a larger group of women gathered by a particular area and thinks, "That must be where all the action is!" and hurries to find out what is happening. As she arrives, she sees that the women have gathered around the impressive dessert display and are all eagerly discussing which sinful indulgence they have their eye on. Wanda spots a piece of chocolate cake that is calling her name and reaches for it just as another woman does the same. Laughing, they decide to split that dessert and another that looks appealing. "There's nothing like chocolate to bring women together," she laughs and thinks about what a good decision this turned out to be.

Same event, same circumstances, two VERY different emotional reactions. To explain this event, I'd like to introduce you to something that you do every day but have probably never heard of...the Reticular Activating System.

Reticular Activating System: Basic Law Of Attraction

I'll explain the how/why/when/where of the system in a minute, but for now, let me show you the result of it. Linda and Tom are in the market for a new car. They drive to the sales lot and begin to look around. An eager salesman takes them to the "Sale of the Day," a blue Jeep Wrangler. Linda and Tom were not really in the market for a Jeep, but decide to take it for a test drive. Both of them have a good time envisioning all of the 4WD adventures they could have and it suddenly becomes an actual option. They decide to go home and think about it. If they still wanted it in a week, they would come back and buy it! A funny thing happened over that week—they see Jeep Wranglers EVERYWHERE. They couldn't believe how many people drove them. Maybe all the dealerships in the area were having a sale on Jeeps, and a bunch of people decided to buy them! After the end of the week, Tom and Linda took all the Jeep sightings "as a sign" and decided to purchase the Jeep.

So, were all the dealerships randomly selling Jeeps that week? Maybe, but not likely. Does this scenario sound familiar? A friend brings up a particular topic at lunch and then for days following, it seems like everyone is talking about it! This well-known phenomenon is simply a bundle of nerves at our brainstem that acts as a filter. It "tunes out" unnecessary information so the important stuff gets through. What is the "important" stuff? Whatever you have been focusing on (thoughts). This system is at work when you can tune out a crowd full of talking people, yet immediately snap to attention when someone says your name. Your Reticular Activating System (RAS) takes what you focus on and creates a filter for it. It then sifts through the filing system and presents only the pieces that are relevant and important to you. Of course, all of this happens without you being aware of it.

Okay, this is big. This is where our thoughts end up dictating what we get more of. Whatever we focus on, we get MORE of. Our brain is engineered to see/feel/know MORE of what we have already deemed important. The RAS seeks information that validates your beliefs. It filters the world through the parameters you give it, and your beliefs shape those parameters. If you believe that you are bad at math, you probably will be. If you believe you are a good friend, you most likely will be. The RAS helps you see what you want to see, and in doing so, influences your actions.

So let's revisit Darla and Wanda to see the RAS at work. Darla walked into the room and spotted a large group of women gathering together. Her mind sorts and filters data from the billions of files held within her subconscious mind. What it finds was a mother who was reclusive and didn't have many close friendships, bullying from a group of "mean girls" in middle school, Facebook posts, Instagram comments of women tearing each other down out of insecurity, and many more bits of information. Darla's RAS has a filter for rejection. So, without her knowledge, her RAS is fine-tuned to finding any *hint* of rejection in any given situation. The problem is, our internal reality becomes our external reality. And remember, we create our own internal reality. So because Darla's subconscious mind came to the conclusion that she was frequently "rejected" growing up, she is exceptionally attuned for looking for it. So, just like the Jeep, guess what Darla finds everywhere. Yep, you guessed it

—rejection. But this is where it gets really interesting; do you see that Darla actually *created* the rejection?

Granted, the group of women were not even aware of Darla. Not one. They were busy ogling the desserts. They were no more "rejecting" her than they were firing semi-automatic rifles in her direction. BUT, that is not what Darla felt. Remember, she caught some of their eyes drifting in her direction and then laughing? In reality, a few of the women were glancing around the room conspiratorially, trying to figure out the number of women they would need to be sharing desserts with. All in good fun, of course. Which led to bouts of laughter. Not one woman even noticed Darla. Even that is part of Darla's creation. When we think thoughts that lead to emotions that produce feelings, our body responds in kind. So as soon as Darla perceived rejection, her body got small and she "shrunk in." Humans have the ability to "blend in" if it is in our best interest. Because of the perceived rejection, Darla didn't want to be seen and her body would have gone through physical changes in alignment with that desire.

In contrast, Wanda's perception of the very same scenario was completely different because her mind did the obligatory scan of the held data to assess the appropriate behavior at that moment, Wanda's mind found experiences where crowds meant collective interest. Wanda's mind found no significant "danger" in a crowd of women gathered together. In fact, to Wanda, this signaled something of interest. Her RAS was attuned to opportunity and gaining knowledge, so she viewed the crowd as a completely different event. Of course, when she arrived, she found just what she had been "looking for."

In *Breaking the Habit of Being Yourself: How to Lose Your Mind and Create a New One* (2012), Joe Dispenza mentions, "We just love the rush of energy from our troubles! In time, we unconsciously become addicted to our problems, our unfavorable circumstances, or our unhealthy relationships."

These automatic reactions are based on emotions that are a result of chemicals interacting with your cells and we can become addicted to the sensations. Yes, even if the sensations are "negative." We become so familiar with our addictive emotions, they start seeming normal.

Let's, for a minute, consider what I am saying is true. Doesn't it change EVERYTHING? It should. This is Mind Change. We need to change our minds about what we *think* about our minds. Whoa!

Perception

I've mentioned the word **perception** numerous times. So I think it is worthy of digging into a bit. What is perception? The word perception is the way the body "takes in" the information from the outside world. According to the Oxford English Dictionary, perception is "the process of becoming aware or conscious of a thing or things in general; the state of being aware; consciousness; understanding." [4] This process requires the use of one or more of the senses in order to process data. To be perceivable, the object must be able to be understood by the mind through the use of sight, sound, taste, touch, and/or smell. To interpret that sensation is what is known as perception. The perceivable is that which can be interpreted by the body. I'm particularly fond of the word's original Latin meaning as "the action of taking possession, apprehension with the mind or senses." Perception is what allows us to make sense of the world through the experience of our senses and the collection of data.

Simply put, perception is how we view the world based on our experience with it. Sound familiar? It goes back to how we form our particular Model of the World. Perception is how we create our personal reality. For example, let's take a bottle of Tabasco. A person will view this bottle and instantly have a *perception* of its meaning. If you are someone who likes spice and heat (how do you know?..you will search your files and find previous experiences to take from), then you will feel feelings of satisfaction. Your mouth may even begin to salivate when you think of the smell or taste. If, on the other hand, you are someone who has a negative association with Tabasco, your *perception* of this bottle will be very different. This person may scrunch up their face and even put a hand on their stomach as memories of heartburn arise from their files.

See, Tabasco isn't *good* or *bad*. It just is. The meaning we give it comes from our own personal experience with it. And our perception becomes our reality. What if someone has never had an experience with Tabasco? What will their perception be? The first thing they would do is search their files to see if they have any similar reference that will help them establish a meaning. Likely, they will use their visual capabilities to assess the look, color, and shape of the bottle. Do they find a familiar shape, look, or color? If nothing is definitive, they may decide to smell it. This will likely trigger a response as they search through their filing system (memories) to see if a similar smell can be found. If they find something that seems familiar, they will use that event and make a perception of the current situation. Let's say that this person finds a similar bottle color and smell in a memory of visiting Mexico with family. It was a great trip, and they used a similar bottle to season some tacos. The tacos were spicy, but it was an enjoyable experience shared with friends and family. The tacos were washed down with Horchata, and it was an overall pleasant experience. This person will *perceive* the bottle of Tabasco as a possible pleasant experience and would likely try it out.

Let's say another person, who is unfamiliar with Tabasco, searches their memory bank to find an associated experience. This person finds a memory of a time when their older sibling and some older cousins pulled a prank on him involving a "special" ice cream topping. The older kids made a big fuss over this "delicious" new topping and convinced the younger boy to try it. Saying it was a fruit topping, they dumped the hot sauce from a bottle onto a bite of vanilla ice cream. Asking the boy to "open wide," the older boys dumped the spoonful of hot sauce-covered ice cream down his throat. Instantly, the boy realized that he had made a grave mistake in trusting these older boys. As he remembers, he can still feel the burn of his throat and tongue. What is his likely conclusion of Tabasco? That is just by seeing the bottle! What if he smelled it as well? Clearly, these "senses" are powerful indicators for us. Even more than that, they are actually the building blocks of what we call memories.

CHAPTER 5

Memory Mis-Education

"I'm interested in memory because it's a filter through which we see our lives, and because it's foggy and obscure, the opportunities for self-deception are there. In the end, as a writer, I'm more interested in what people tell themselves happened rather than what actually happened."

Kazuo Ishiguro

Memory Mis-Education

Our society and culture regard memories as sacred ground. We often give irrevocable authority to our memories, therefore believing that something remembered is something true. Because we have the common belief that "seeing is believing," it stands to reason that if 60% of the population holds their memories visually, a vast majority of us will believe the picture our mind gives us regarding a past event.

Very often, we also feel an enormous pressure to remember. Especially during traumatic events. The horrific events of 9/11 spawned the famous catchphrase "Never Forget." Veteran's Day asks us to "Never Forget" the soldiers who have died for our freedom. Elie Wiesel, speaking of the Holocaust in his 1986 Nobel Peace Prize lecture, said "Like the body, memory protects its wounds." [1] Added later in his same lecture, Wiesel said, "And yet it is surely human to forget, even to want to forget. The Ancients saw it as a divine gift. Indeed if memory helps us to survive, forgetting allows us to go on living. How could we go on with our daily lives, if we remained constantly aware of the dangers and ghosts surrounding us?" (Wiesel, 1986). Yes, memory is a sacred thing.

Most of us assume that what we remember is accurate. And we have learned that events are recorded and encoded into our brains using 1 or more of our 5 senses. But where we make the mistake is in believing that when we *recall* those memories, they *show* in exactly the same way they were encoded.

Elizabeth Loftus, a contemporary psychologist, is one of the foremost experts in memory. In her research, Loftus and her colleagues demonstrated that questions asked after a person witnesses an event can actually *have an influence* on the person's recollection of that event [2]. If a question contains misleading information, it can distort the memory of the event, a phenomenon that psychologists have dubbed the misinformation effect. Loftus explained,

"The misinformation effect refers to the impairment in memory for the past that arises after exposure to misleading information." [3]

I highly recommend viewing her TED Talk, "How Reliable Is Your Memory?" Focusing specifically on *false memories*, Loftus clearly shows just how easy it is to distort or alter reality through the filter of our memory. Another powerful example of this phenomenon was fodder for the 1980s 20/20 investigation done by ABC News entitled, "Can You Always Believe The Children?" This program highlights a time in the 1980s where daycare child abuse claims were skyrocketing.

One such case was the McMartin Preschool Trial. This case focused on the McMartin Preschool in Manhattan Beach, California, where seven teachers were accused of kidnapping children, flying them in a plane to another location, and forcing them to engage in group sex as well as forcing them to watch animals be tortured and killed. The case also involved accusations that children had been forced to participate in bizarre religious rituals and had been used to make child pornography [4]. The case began with a single accusation made by a mother of one of the students (who was later found to be a paranoid schizophrenic). Accusations grew rapidly when investigators started informing parents and began interviewing other students [5].

The case made headlines nationwide in 1984, and seven teachers were arrested and charged that year. However, when a new district attorney took over the case in 1986, his office re-examined the evidence and dropped charges against all but two of the original defendants. This became one of the most protracted and most expensive criminal trials in the history of the United States, but in 1990, all of these charges were also dropped. Both jurors and academic researchers at the trial later criticized the interviewing techniques that investigators used in their investigations of the school, alleging that interviewers had "coaxed" children into making unfounded accusations, repeatedly asking children the same questions and offering various incentives until the children reported having been abused. Most scholars now agree that the accusations these interviews elicited from children were false [6].

Clearly, both of these examples mention "misleading" information from outside sources as causes of these memory malfunctions. But what if the most signifiant source of misleading information is actually...us?

What Is A Memory?

We are going to revisit this idea of perception in a little more detail later on. But for now, let's focus on memory. What do you think of when you think of a memory? Depending on what you are thinking about, it could appear in different forms. A picture, a feeling, a sound, or a smell. It can even be a "knowing" that something happened. If we didn't have memories, we'd just be a body. We wouldn't be able to communicate, to love, to laugh, or even identify danger. We would be oblivious to how to survive in the world around us.

Memory is crucial in transforming us from helpless newborns into capable adults. Up to this point, I have been referring to "files" in our filing system. The more familiar terminology for this is the word "memory." So what is a memory? Scientifically, a memory is the result of processing stimuli with the neuronal activity that encodes, stores, and retrieves experiences and knowledge into various regions of the brain. But for our purposes, we are going to look at it a little more simplistically. We've already talked a lot about how much our memories (files) shape our thoughts, actions, and behaviors. Remember, we can only "out"put what we have "in"put. So let's take a closer look at how we "in"put.

How Do We Build A Memory?

You were probably introduced to the idea of "The 5 Senses" in middle school biology. You were likely taught that we have 5 basic senses: sight, feeling (touch), hearing, smell, and taste. For our purposes, we are going to dive a little deeper into these. I learned the majority of what I'm about to describe to you by studying NLP. NLP is short for Neuro-Linguistic Programming. Dr. Matt James of NLP.com defines it like this, "NLP stands for Neuro-Linguistic Programming. Neuro refers to your neurology; Linguistic refers to language; programming refers to how that neural language functions. In other words, learning NLP is like learning the language of your own mind!"

NLP refers to these as the Representational Systems and uses the terms Visual (what we see), Audio (what we hear), Kinesthetic (what we feel), Audio Digital (words that we say to ourselves/knowings), Olfactory (smell), and Gustatory (taste). As we take in information from any of these senses, the brain uniquely encodes that information. The term

"Representational Systems" comes from the observation that we will *re*-present our memories from one of these modes. Studies have shown that humans primarily use the Visual, Auditory, and Kinesthetic systems. In America, approximately 20% of people process strongly Auditory, 20% do so Kinesthetically, and 60% do so Visually. Because a large percentage of the population primarily uses the Visual system, many people think of memory as a picture in your head. That is not always the case.

For instance, if I were to tell you to close your eyes and remember your childhood home, some of you would produce a *picture* of that home in your mind. That is the visual representation of that memory. Someone else might get a warm and safe *feeling*, remembering what it *felt* like in the home. This is a kinesthetic representation. Yet another person may *hear* the familiar sounds of dishes being washed, or the symphony of voices at the dinner table, or even the neighborhood kids playing outside. This is an auditory representation. They are all "memory."

Different memories may have been encoded in different ways. You may remember your childhood dog with a picture, but your first bike with the feeling of the wind going through your hair. You can also have many or all of the senses represented in one memory. You may remember your childhood pet with a picture or movie inside your head, the feeling of his fur under your hand and the warm, loving feeling you got from being with him. This is all memory! See the diagram here.

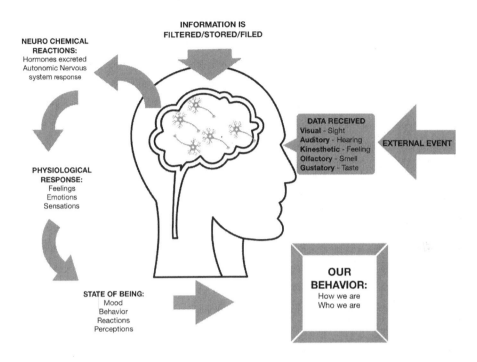

Why is this important? Because it's helpful to understand that by simply pulling up a picture, feeling, or sound from our head, we can be *feeling* those feelings NOW, just as if the event was happening to us at this very moment. This can be a good thing, but also a terrifying and horrible thing. Why? Because we can see something or we experience *sensations* and *feelings* simply by recalling something from our past; we feel that our memories are "real." This common misunderstanding about the way we perceive reality can definitely shape the way we see memories.

Revisiting A Memory Changes It

A study conducted at Northwestern University [7] concluded that every time you remember an event from the past, your brain's networks change in ways that can alter the later recall of the event. Meaning, the next time you remember it, you might not recall the original event but rather what you remembered the previous time. In a landmark 2010 paper in Nature, Daniela Schiller (then a postdoc at New York University) and her NYU colleagues published the results of human experiments indicating that memories are reshaped and rewritten every time we recall an event [8].

So, it turns out that the *recall* process of our memory is a lot like playing the Telephone Game with ourselves. You know the old game? You start with one sentence and then whisper it quietly into the ear of the person sitting next to you. This goes on until the sentence has been passed from person to person in a circle. When it comes back to the originator of the sentence, it is said aloud. More often than not, the sentence at the end barely resembles the original sentence. The more people you have, the sillier the game gets.

If we fundamentally (and unknowingly) change our memories every time we revisit them, what does that mean about our memories? They cannot be relied upon to portray the "truth" of any situation. Research shows that memory is elastic and malleable. If you think about it, it makes sense to realize that we cannot access information from our past and recall it with the exact same thoughts, feelings, and ideas that we encoded it with —simply because we are not the same person from one day to the next!

For example, I worked with a client who was revisiting a memory of childhood trauma. This event took place when she was 3 years old, but she had very vivid pictures and feelings surrounding this event. As I asked more questions, it was clear that this particular memory was one that had been accessed and revisited countless times over a 30-year period. She had done extensive talk therapy around this trauma and was well versed in every aspect of this memory. At one point, I asked her to go back and *feel the feelings* of that little 3-year-old girl. When I asked what she believed the little girl had been feeling, she quickly gave me a few complex and articulate feelings. "She felt violated, manipulated, and worthless."

I don't doubt for one second that my client was *experiencing* feelings of violation, manipulation, and worthlessness as she sat in my office recalling the memory. But I also know that a typical 3-year-old simply wouldn't and couldn't possess the emotional wherewithal to express such complex feelings and emotions. See, she was recalling that memory and *changing* it every time it was recalled. A 3-year-old child cannot understand or feel the emotion of "manipulation" because they have absolutely no context for it. But a 33-year-old woman would...and did. Over the years, this individual had used these memories to define her and therefore was very skilled in the language of a sexual abuse victim. She didn't do this purposefully or even knowingly. Over the years, she developed the vocabulary and the Emotional Intelligence to project those complex emotions onto that 3-year-old girl.

See, our brain automatically rewrites details of our memories to support our current view of ourselves and our life story *now*. It's been said that our memories are like Swiss cheese; with "holes" that we try to fill each time it is recalled [9]. And we try to fill those up with related information or new insights into our learning. It may be more accurate to say they are more like American cheese or Velveeta—full of synthetic fillers so that you get something that *resembles* cheese, but isn't really. Since what we remember changes each time we recall the event, the slightly-changed memory is now embedded as "real," only to be reconstructed with the next recall. We are completely unaware of this happening.

So if memory is like a file in our brain, we have to see that the file data is edited every time it is accessed. At each re-telling or re-visiting, there are attached emotional or visual details. When the data is altered, the output or behavior that is produced is also reshaped.

Now before you have an existential crisis, let me remind you of how you *already* know this to be true. Have you ever been sitting around with family or a group of friends that are retelling an event or experience you all shared in? Everyone begins to tell *their* version of what happened. Each person is ABSOLUTELY POSITIVE it happened the way *they* remember it. Sometimes, if the story is retold enough, a friend or family member who *wasn't even actually at the event* begins chiming in with details that *they* remember from the event. At times, it can be comical. In marriages and families, this can be quite a frustration!

Let me offer another example. A woman, who we will call Barb, comes to see me for trichotillomania (hair-pulling). Since she was a teenager, Barb has been pulling out her hair compulsively, and it has significantly altered her life. Through some strategic questioning, we land on an interesting belief. "I have bad hair." When I ask Barb how she *knows* she has "bad hair" and when the earliest memory she has of this knowing, she finds a memory dating back to elementary school. At 8 years old, Barb remembers her mother angrily pulling her hair up into "tight, painful" ponytails on a daily basis. Upon further investigation into this memory, Barb remembers her mom seeming angry and frustrated at the task of managing Barbs long and "unmanageable" hair. "My mother never liked my hair," Barb stated emphatically. "It was always a burden and bother to her, and I think she has always resented me because of it."

After a short time, we connected that Barb would often pull her hair at times of insecurity. She often felt like a burden to other people and would resort to hair pulling to relieve the pressure of that negative feeling. Using the Mind Change techniques, we worked through many of these negative belief patterns and programs in her mind.

After our first session, I felt that we had made a good deal of progress. The next day, I receive a seemingly frantic email from Barb that I needed to contact her right away. Thinking that our session had likely uncovered more areas that were demanding attention, I called her. "You are not going to believe this," Barb said. She was clearly in quite a state and I braced myself for what she was about to say. "I called my mother last night and happened to mention the memory of her torturing me with those ponytails when I was little. I let her know I was making peace with her dislike of my hair and the burden that I had felt like I was to her." Barb eagerly continued, "And do you know what she says to me? She tells me that she never disliked my hair. In fact, she loved my hair and thought I had the most beautiful hair she had ever seen. When I asked her about the horrible ponytails that she made me wear every day because she hated my hair, she was completely shocked. She said that the reason she did the ponytails was because my school was constantly having lice breakouts and she never wanted me to get it! She said one of my little friends had gotten it and had to cut off her long hair and it was so traumatic for her. My mother said she loved my hair so much, and never wanted me to have to suffer through that." I sat on the other end of the phone smiling as she went on, "When I asked her why she was always so angry, my mom said she wasn't angry, she was just worried and wanted to help keep me safe so that I could keep my beautiful hair."

Barb and her mother shared a good laugh but also shared some tears. Neither of them could have imagined that memory would have contributed to the years of pain from the trichotillomania. When Barb and I spoke again, she asked how things could have gone so wrong. I explained that we input memories with the skills we have at the time. Little children are not very adept at deciphering the complex emotions of adults. They will generally default to "it's my fault" and feel that they have done something "bad" or "wrong" to deserve this behavior. As an 8-year-old child, Barb couldn't have possibly understood that her mothers "anger" was actually anxiety and fear. As an 8-year-old, Barb reasoned like an 8-year-old. That's all she could do.

On the other hand, Barb's mother couldn't have possibly known that Barb thought she was angry or resentful or that Barb was a burden. As adults, we often mask our core emotions with more manageable, surface emotions. Children find these difficult to read and have not been trained (yet) to read between the lines.

The next time I saw Barb, her hair had grown out beautifully, and she had it up in a high ponytail. She no longer used hair pulling as a coping skill. Now, every time she remembers or sees a ponytail, it brings up feelings of love and protection. It reminds her of how beautiful her hair was (and is) and gives her a feeling of love. Even better, she knows that it's not the *ponytail* creating the love feeling, it's the memory of her mother's care and devotion. Now, when she revisits these memories, she sees her mother's smile and her own beautiful and shiny hair. Rather than torture, the ponytail feels comforting and protective. You see, her memory *changed* with the new perspective she was able to get. It's interesting how many people are defined by childhood abuse and trauma. And yet, those definitions are limited to the small range of understanding and emotion that we possessed as children.

For the past 6 years, I have witnessed this phenomenon of memory rewriting in myself and my clients. In Part 2, I'll explain in more detail how we do this. But for now, you need to wrap your head around the fact that it's possible. As science catches up with what I already know to be true, that memory is subjective and pliable, many exciting studies are emerging. In The Ted Talk, "A Mouse. A Laser Beam. A Manipulated Memory" Steve Ramirez and Xu Liu of MIT explain their experience with memory manipulation in the brains of mice. The conclusion states that memories, and more specifically, the *details* of memories, can be purposefully manipulated to produce a chosen behavior.

As the world attempts to "life-hack" their way to health and happiness, this information allows us to go right to the source of our current problems (how they were created) and redecorate! Can you imagine the implications? The narrative of movies like *Inception* and *Eternal*

Sunshine of the Spotless Mind no longer seem like far-fetched science fiction.

For us, this simply means that no matter what was *input* into the filing system of the mind that goes on to dictate our thoughts, feelings and behaviors...we can go in and intentionally remove or change any information that doesn't serve or support what we want to be, feel, and think—NOW. We are "mind architects," if we choose to be. We get to "let go" of what is not working in our lives and "put in" the skills and outcomes we do want. We have the power to design and build an emotionally-fulfilling life by the experiences we choose to have and memories we encode in our brains. This is why I believe this information and knowledge needs to be spread to the world.

If this is true (which I hope you believe now), then why are so many people still miserable? Dr. Caroline Leaf states that research shows that 75-98% of all mental physical and behavioral illness comes from one's thought life [10]. There is a paradox to this power that we all possess. **What we think about the most, we get more of**. Remember the RAS (Reticular Activating System)? Depending on what we think about the most, and what memories from our past that we are using as references, this power will either produce "good" results or "not so good" results.

Emotional Intelligence

Emotional Intelligence is one of the latest health and wellness "buzz words" though it first came to light in the 90s. Emotional Intelligence can be defined as an ability to monitor your own emotions as well as the emotions of others, to distinguish between and label different emotions correctly, and to use emotional information to guide your thinking and behavior and influence that of others. According to Daniel Goleman, there are five components or elements of Emotional Intelligence [11]:

- Self-Awareness
- Self-Regulation
- Motivation
- Empathy
- Social Skills

Rather than go deeply into this framework, I want to highlight something true for a large number of us. Emotional Intelligence is a skill. One that has to be taught, learned, and then mastered. From my experience, not many of us naturally possess this skill. And neither did our parents! In fact, until recently, our culture viewed emotions and feelings as bothersome byproducts of life rather than a way to intentionally produce our lives. Remember, at birth, the brain is a blank slate awaiting "wiring instructions" from a caregiver. If those caregivers are, themselves, not trained or equipped to identify different emotions, how can that skill possibly be passed down?

In fact, I think we are far better trained and practiced at *feeling* one thing and *portraying* another. As adults, we can make excuses for this behavior and reason through it. But for children, they have not yet learned this ability and are left to navigate a world of muted or duplicitous emotions. In the end, they finally learn to do the same. In the next chapter, we will look at how this plays out in our lives and in our genetic expression.

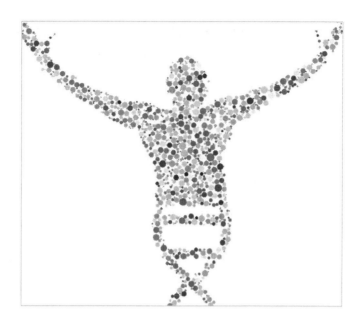

CHAPTER 6

Trauma: It's In The Genes

Trauma is a highly personal thing. What is "traumatic" for one person, might seem trivial to another. We often judge one another's experiences through our own personal lenses, and trauma cannot be approached in this way. What we do know is that most people *have* experienced trauma in their lives, and as a society, we have been grossly under-equipped in how to deal with it. In fact, we have become experts at *not* dealing with trauma. Instead, we "cope."

We often equate "not feeling it" or "not thinking about it" as dealing with something. If it doesn't bother me, it doesn't exist. The problem is that it doesn't "bother" us because we simply don't acknowledge it. The "it" being our unpleasant feelings, experiences, thoughts, or past. This is the way I handled my past for the majority of my life. I could easily speak about the abuse, the neglect, and the trauma. I would routinely say that I was no longer bothered with it. "The past is in the past. You can't change it, so why think about it." This was really my mantra for daily living.

Consciously, we can avoid thinking about those negative experiences. But subconsciously, they are alive and well and usually gaining momentum. Remember, it's our *subconscious* that dictates our daily thoughts, attitudes, and behaviors. It's automatic. The inevitable *out*-put of what we have *in*-put over time. But we have settled for simply "not thinking about it" and considering that a victory. Now, I am NOT saying it's a victory to be in constant thought about the negative experiences of our lives. That is emotional suicide. What I am saying is that we shouldn't settle for just being okay on the outside. Ideally, we clean up the inside, and the outside will reflect that.

If you have seen the show *Hoarders*, you will understand this concept. People don't start out as hoarders. It's an accumulation. And it always has a deeper motivation than "having more stuff." Often times, you don't know someone is a hoarder from the *outside* of the house. It's only when you open the door that it becomes apparent. But left alone for a period of time, the "hoard" cannot be kept in, and it starts to "leak out." First, it's the closet, then the house, then the garage, then the yard. People often notice an unpleasant smell coming from the property, or see increased pest activity like cockroaches or rats. This is a lot like our minds. We are very concerned with the *outside* of the house looking good, but often at the expense of the inside.

Coping Mechanisms: Keeping In The Hoard

We are expert avoiders. And one of the key ways that we avoid is with coping mechanisms. In fact, we have turned coping into a TRILLION dollar business. To *feel* good, we have to *look* good. So the fitness and beauty industries thrive. We are so busy giving our power away to the things, people, and situations that make us feel bad that we employ the *same* tactic to feel better.

If I find the right diet, lifestyle, job, mate, body, hobby...etc., I will *feel* good. If I can find a successful career, I will overcome the feelings I had about growing up poor. If I have the right body or beauty, I will find the right partner. If I can find the right partner, I will overcome the knowledge that nobody ever loved me for me. We give our power away and feel *bad*, then we give it away again to feel *good*. I think you have probably witnessed that this doesn't work. It's never enough. Why? We believe the power to have a good life is outside of us. Truth is, it has always been inside of us.

We are cope-aholics. We don't want to *feel*. We work, play, read, exercise, Facebook, Instagram, have sex, eat, join support groups, watch TV...anything to keep us busy and distracted from the reality that we are not satisfied with our lives. Or we keep the expectations *so low* that we could never really be disappointed because we never really expected much.

Eating is good, vital even. But we do it to *feel* better. Acting like there is actually love in that chocolate bar or donut. Working out is great. But what are we running from? Work is necessary and fulfilling at times. But do we use it to escape and stay busy? God forbid we should get quiet for a few minutes. What would your mind do? What thoughts might arise? What feelings would creep to the surface? Most of us cannot risk it.

For some of us, like the hoarders, the "mess" looks too big. That is if you were to really look to see what has become of your home. Most hoarders have small little pathways throughout their house. Around them, trash and accumulated "stuff" towers over them on each side of the path. Entire rooms or wings of the house are blocked completely. We look at that and are horrified that people would have built such walls of rubbish around them, that they only follow narrow little paths to one or two rooms of their house. But how many of us mentally live that same way? We have "packed away" so much rubbish from our lives mentally and emotionally that there are only a few little areas that are safe.

You will recognize these people. They find offense in everything. If you dare tread outside of the "safe" zones, it's like their very life is in danger, and they will attack. Don't mention the smell. Or the strange oozing of emotions that don't seem to "fit" the situation. Their inner world is so precariously constructed that one mis-step could bring it all down. Seem extreme? How many of us wake up in the morning at the same time, get up and pee in the same toilet, shuffle out and drink the same coffee out of the same cup. Get ready in the same order, brush our teeth with the same hand, think the same thoughts, and drive to work the same way. Work with the same people, have the same conversations, eat at the same place. Drive home at the same time, eat dinner and watch the same shows on TV, check our email, Facebook, Instagram to see "what's new." Feel the same feelings as we browse and go to bed at the same time, just so we can wake up and do the same thing tomorrow.

For some people, this sounds divine. That order, reliability, control. For others, this sounds horrible (though they do some variation of it themselves). There is some comfort in this. A schedule, a plan. The problem is, we often use this as a way to manage what's going on inside of us. To carefully keep the "mess" at bay. And there is comfort in the well traveled little paths that we have created. We know what's "safe" and what to expect. The problem is, most of us are not truly happy. And this isn't "life." It's routine and doesn't challenge our minds to grow beyond what we already know.

But what if we weren't carefully trying to contain our "mess"? What if we were adventurers? Even at the same house, at the same job? I'll explain more about that later, but I bet you can imagine that things would look and feel a lot different. So what keeps us stuck? Trauma.

The Survival Loop: How Trauma Keeps Us Stuck

Dr. Peter Levine, the creator of Somatic Experiencing®, is a leading expert in our body's response to trauma. Observing animals in the wild, Dr. Levine noticed that animals who had experienced a perceived life-threatening trauma would have a strange "whole body" shaking once they had reached safety [1]. In his video, "Nature's Lessons in Healing Trauma: An Introduction to Somatic Experiencing" [2], you can see an example with a polar bear. It has been recognized that this whole body tremor effect is the physical release and elimination of all the "trauma" experienced from the event. In fact, Dr. David Berceli developed a technique called TRE based on this tremoring [3].

For instance, let's say a gazelle happens to escape the jaws of a lioness and finds itself in safety. You will witness a process that this animal will go through to release and discharge this experience from its body. This process happens in stages. Research has shown that if animals are not able to complete this process, they risk debilitating effects on their health, even death. They were not actually mortally harmed by the attack itself, but from the effects of the trauma on the mind/body. A great example of this is in a youtube video entitled "Impala escaping an attack" [4] (Warning: graphic images).

Clearly, trauma has effects and consequences that go beyond just "feeling" scared. Humans usually do not do this trauma discharge. Not only are we taught to "suck it up" or "be strong," we aren't aware that there is anything we *can* do about it. Severe shaking and coming back *through* the trauma does not seem like a logical or safe option to our thinking brain. In fact, as children, we are taught NOT to act out when we feel strong emotions, so we don't have to feel. But seeing this process play out in the animal kingdom makes it clear that we might be missing something with regard to trauma processing. Matt Schwenteck of TRE says, "only two kinds of mammals have forgotten how to do this life-saving tremoring: zoo animals and humans." [5]

The Science Of Survival

Trauma has an impact on the entire human system. The brain, mind, and body all process this event with different systems and responses. This cycle is complex and intricate.

In my opinion, Dr. Bessel Van Der Kolk, author of *The Body Keeps Score*, is one of the foremost experts in the field of trauma on the human body. A professor of Psychiatry at Boston University School of Medicine, he did some of the leading research in PTSD patients [6]. Dr. Van Der Kolk explains that we are pre-programmed with a "brain alarm system" that automatically triggers when we perceive or encounter threat. This engages the oldest part of the brain, the Reptilian Brain. When the Reptilian Brain is in control, it partially shuts down the higher brain, our PreFrontal Cortex or Neo Cortex, our rational or thinking brain. It generally has three basic responses; fight, flight, or freeze [7].

In response to acute stress, the amygdala gland becomes activated. The amygdala's job is to determine whether the current event is a threat. It does this in a less than a millisecond based on sensory input that we are not even consciously aware of. To help make the decision, it engages the hippocampus, which is where all the "file folders" (memories) are stored. It scans through past experiences to help identify possible threats. If the amygdala decides that a possible threat is present, it engages the body's autonomic nervous system, which triggers a sudden release of hormones. The sympathetic nervous systems stimulate the adrenal glands, thereby triggering the release of catecholamines, which include cortisol, adrenaline, and noradrenaline. These hormones trigger our body to respond in various ways and results in a whole-body response. Our senses are heightened, our heart will beat faster, we can have moments of increased strength or speed. We are actually built to go "super-human" for brief moments of time to help us stay alive! This is an AMAZING system! But we are not meant to stay in that state for any real length of time.

Functioning "normally," the most evolved part of our brain, the Pre-Frontal Cortex plays a vital role in this process. While the Amygdala gland is ready to "take action" at the first sign of danger, our frontal lobes can restore peace in our systems if it deems the threat a "false alarm." For instance, you are in a city park with your children when you suddenly hear tires screeching. Before you are consciously aware of it, you have jumped to your feet and moved toward your child. When you regain awareness (thank you frontal lobes), you realize that the street is nowhere close to the park and your child is safe. Likely, you settle down quickly and take a few deep breaths, even able to find your reaction humorous. With your PreFrontal Cortex back in control, you have consciously assessed the situation and decided you and your child were not in danger. The amygdala is quieted, released little to no hormones, making it easier to come back to homeostasis (normal).

The problem is, with each use, each system gets stronger. "Practice makes perfect." Our Pre-Frontal Cortex helps us be mindful of our situations, seeing different possible perspectives before reacting or making decisions. It helps us understand that *other people's* emotions are a state of *their* well being and have little to do with us personally. It helps us have deep and meaningful relationships with those around us as we can observe our own thoughts and feelings. This system allows us to patiently apply the brakes in the car when someone pulls out in front of us and assuming the other driver simply did not see us.

The same is with the Amygdala gland. If it has been overly engaged, especially as a child, it can become accustomed to "taking control." Research has shown that repeated trauma, or what I call PNEs (perceived negative experiences), can increase the sensitivity of the amygdala gland. This increases the risk that situations will be interpreted as dangerous. Even small "glitches" in this system can lead to relationship turmoil. You sense that your partner might be angry with you, and from past negative experiences, you quickly engage your "fight back" response. Unfortunately, the frontal lobes are "off-line" which doesn't allow you to think clearly at all. When the "thinking/reasoning" part of our brain is inhibited, we are left to our primal responses and actions. This is where tempers suddenly flare and become unpredictable over the slightest thing. Or someone may completely freeze and/or withdraw when being put on the spot. Fear has been practiced so often that it is the "go-to" response to keep the body safe.

Neuroimaging studies of the brain in PTSD sufferers shows significantly increased activity in the subcortical regions of the brain [8]. The areas that regulate fear, sadness, pain, and anger are more active, and they seem "stuck" in the emotional brain. After a trauma, especially repeated trauma, the nervous system responds differently. This can cause an increase in hormone production, keeping the body in a constant state of low-level reactivity. Now, the body must reroute precious energy and focus in order to suppress the "hair trigger" reactions. When this person lashes out in pain, fear, or anger out of context, this can cause further trauma and withdrawal. Because the person is stuck in the emotional brain, they rarely engage the pre-frontal region to get a "higher perspective." This becomes a vicious cycle. Now every new experience is tainted by the perpetual state of looking for, and reacting to, trauma. The body is forced to defend itself daily against a threat that is being produced by the mind. The constant vigilance and energy it takes to maintain this cycle can take a hefty emotional and physical toll on the body.

PNEs - Perceived Negative Experiences

Remember, trauma is subjective. Even though we all possess the same basic "warning and response system," the way we *in*-put the experience, as well as our unique model of the world, will be big factors in how this experience is filed. Also, our individual perceptions of trauma are different. A child could be yelled at by a teacher in school, and depending on this child's previous experiences, this could be devastating or largely ignored. Even children raised in the same home can have vastly different reactions to the same experiences.

It is my opinion that most of us hold some form of trauma. We all have some experience in our life that continues to haunt us. Granted, someone who felt like they were a bit ignored as a child may not have the same outward effects that a survivor of incest may exhibit, but the hurt is there nonetheless. Our society is good at comparing. And we often gauge our suffering by the suffering of others.

"Well, at least I didn't have it *that* bad."

"Yeah, my father wasn't around much, but at least he didn't beat me."

"I was bullied terribly in school...but wasn't everyone?"

"My mother was an alcoholic, but not as bad as other people I know."

At first glance, these statements seem like the better of two options. You know the other one, the "woe is me...I had it worse than anyone" type of person. The trouble is, both of these people are hurting. They both have had hurtful, negative experiences, but the latter type tends to get the worse reputation. Of course, we can see why. Most of us are just trying to keep all those negative memories, thoughts, and emotions at bay on a daily basis. We don't need some "poor me" individual constantly reminding us of just how fragile our own grip is on "normal."

What if we have another option? What if we each can acknowledge our own hurts and experiences, but rather than broadcasting them day and night, or stuffing them down into the subconscious abyss, or denying them altogether....what if we could actually deal with them?

It is my belief that nearly all dis-ease in the body and mind comes from one thing: Perceived Negative Experiences. Unfortunately, no amount of positive thought, positive affirmations, yoga, drugs, booze, sex, or makeup can cover these up forever. Some of these things will seem to help, even for long stretches of time. But it always shows up somewhere. In the book, *Feelings Buried Alive Never Die*, Karol K. Truman explains that most, if not all, of the problems we face in life, are because of unresolved feelings [9]. As discussed in Chapter 4, we know that feelings are just chemical responses to our memories.

As much as we would like to keep "the past in the past," if there are PNEs that need to be processed and resolved, they will keep showing up to be resolved. I will discuss this in more length soon, but the important thing to realize is that if *we* are producing and holding these negative experiences, *we* can also decide and learn to let them go! The power is in our hands.

The ACEs Study

In the mental health field, many terms have been coined to try and categorize the seemingly increasing amount of "troubled behavior" in children and adults. Terms like PTSD (post-traumatic stress disorder), DMDD (disruptive mood dysregulation disorder), DID (dissociative identity disorder), DTS (developmental trauma disorder), and on and on.

From 1995 to 1997, Vincent Felitti and Robert Anda, in partnership with the Centers for Disease Control and Prevention (CDC) and Kaiser Permanente, conducted a groundbreaking study in childhood trauma. Over 17,000 participants receiving physical exams completed confidential surveys regarding their childhood experiences, and their current health status and behaviors [10].

This study was inspired by the alarming dropout rate of participants at Kaiser Permanente's obesity clinic in San Diego, California. The dropout rate was about 50%, despite the fact that all of the dropouts had successfully lost weight using the program. Vincent Felitti, head of Kaiser Permanente's Department of Preventive Medicine in San Diego, conducted interviews with people who had left the program, and discovered that a majority of 286 people he interviewed had experienced childhood sexual abuse. Felitti concluded that weight gain might be a coping mechanism for depression, anxiety, and fear.

The ACEs Study found:

ACEs are common. For example, 28% of study participants reported physical abuse, and 21% reported sexual abuse. Many also reported experiencing a divorce or parental separation or having a parent with a mental and/or substance use disorder.

ACEs cluster. Almost 40% of the Kaiser sample reported two or more ACEs and 12.5% experienced four or more. Because ACEs cluster, many subsequent studies now look at the cumulative effects of ACEs rather than the individual effects of each.

ACEs have a dose-response relationship with many health problems. As researchers followed participants over time, they discovered that a person's cumulative ACEs score has a strong, graded relationship to numerous health, social, and behavioral problems throughout their lifespan, including substance use disorders. Furthermore, many problems related to ACEs tend to be comorbid or co-occurring.

The ACE study graphic below shows that our negative childhood experiences are literally killing us [11].

All ACE questions refer to the respondent's first 18 years of life.

Abuse

• Emotional abuse: A parent, stepparent, or adult living in your home swore at you, insulted you, put you down, or acted in a way that made you afraid that you might be physically hurt.

• Physical abuse: A parent, stepparent, or adult living in your home pushed, grabbed, slapped, threw something at you, or hit you so hard that you had marks or were injured.

• Sexual abuse: An adult, relative, family friend, or stranger who was at least 5 years older than you touched or fondled your body in a sexual way, made you touch his/her body in a sexual way, attempted to have any type of sexual intercourse with you.

Household Challenges

• Mother treated violently: Your mother or stepmother was pushed, grabbed, slapped, had something thrown at her, kicked, bitten, hit with a fist, hit with something hard, repeatedly hit for over at least a few minutes, or was ever threatened or hurt by a knife or gun by your father (or stepfather) or mother's boyfriend.

• Household substance abuse: A household member was a problem drinker or alcoholic or a household member used street drugs.

• Mental illness in household: A household member was depressed or mentally ill or a household member attempted suicide.

• Parental separation or divorce: Your parents were ever separated or divorced.

• Criminal household member: A household member went to prison.

Neglect

• Emotional neglect: No one in your family helped you feel important or special, or loved. Members of your family did not look out for each other or feel close to each other.

• Physical neglect: There was no one to take care of you, protect you, and take you to the doctor if you needed it. You didn't have enough to eat, your parents were too drunk or too high to take care of you, and/or you had to wear dirty clothes.

As the number of ACEs increases, so does the risk for the following:

• Alcoholism and alcohol abuse

• Chronic obstructive pulmonary disease

- Depression
- Fetal death
- Health-related quality of life
- Illicit drug use
- Ischemic heart disease
- Liver disease
- Poor work performance
- Financial stress
- Risk for intimate partner violence
- Multiple sexual partners
- Sexually transmitted diseases
- Smoking
- Suicide attempts
- Unintended pregnancies
- Early initiation of smoking
- Early initiation of sexual activity
- Adolescent pregnancy
- Risk of sexual violence
- Poor academic achievement

This body of work calls these experiences ACEs (Adverse Childhood Experiences). I have chosen to use the term PNEs (Perceived Negative Experiences). The reason being, I believe that ACEs will inevitably lead to PNEs. As our child-brain is building its filing system (memory), it is also building the system of *how* we remember. A child with numerous ACEs, will not only repeatedly activate the fight/flight/freeze response, but they will also become increasingly "primal" in their responses and reactions...to any stimulus. When our biological system keeps pumping out stress hormones to deal with threats in a desire to be "ahead of the threat," the child will begin to *perceive* threat.

A physically abused child will instinctively pull away from a well-meaning hug, primally responding to an advancement that usually leads to pain. Though we do learn to manage our response better as we become adults, the "trigger" is still there. Because we learn to *perceive* threat, we begin to accumulate "proof" that we are never really safe. Remember the RAS (Reticular Activating System)? What we focus on, we get more of. To illustrate how a PNE carries over into adulthood, I will share a story of my client, Max.

MAX:

Max* was referred to me because of chronic tinnitus (ringing in the ears). Max had been to conventional doctors, acupuncturists, chiropractors, and even psychiatric therapists. Nothing seemed to help the constant ringing. Max said it was so bad that he wished he could be deaf so that he would hear nothing. But he was fearful that he would go deaf but still "hear" the ringing. His body obliged and he had begun to experience hearing loss and had almost no hearing in his left ear. Max wasn't very hopeful that I could help him.

I reviewed the document he had sent me, listing any traumatic events in his life. Max listed a few things that he could remember but expressed that he felt like his life was pretty good. I did notice the death of a sister around the onset of the symptoms and made a note to dig into that when we met.

Max was a handsome and successful businessman. He had a loving wife and a very active and full social life. But over the last 3 years that he had been suffering from tinnitus, he had begun to pull away from everything.

As we worked together, I noticed that Max exhibited a common trait of those who experience tinnitus—a lack of personal boundaries. Of course, I am aware that Max learned this behavior somewhere in this life and we explored his childhood a bit more. Eventually, I discovered that Max had grown up in a rather tumultuous home. Max's father had left home when he was quite young and his mother was not around much. When she was around, his mother tended to be hostile and verbally abusive. As the oldest of 4 children, Max felt a great responsibility for his brothers and sisters. As with many abusive home environments, children become enmeshed in unhealthy relationships with caregivers. Max often felt like he was trying to keep everything together but always ended up with the blame. As the siblings grew older, Max's younger sister turned to drugs and alcohol to cope. For years, Max felt guilty and responsible for his sister's addiction. Though Max moved to another state, got married and built a successful business, he was constantly trying to keep his extended family together and "help" with whatever the current crisis was.

Sadly, Max's sister, deep into her addiction cycle, decided to take her own life. The responsibility for the preparations and funeral fell solely to Max. During this intimate memorial, the evening before the funeral, Max's mother and siblings (fueled by grief and alcohol) began a very vocal attack on Max. They blamed him for the death of his sister and the devastated remains of the family. At that moment, Max stopped listening. As an effort to protect himself, he completely cut ties with his family from that moment on, and he stopped listening to anything. Though he stopped listening to the insults and abuse (which was good), he also stopped listening to himself and his own judgments (which was not good). When he cut off all communication with his extended family, he also, in effect, cut off communication with himself. Two years later, the "silence" was deafening. One day he woke up with tinnitus and it had been increasing in intensity ever since.

Also common with tinnitus is a rigid and unbending belief system. Because they were so mistreated by the ones that they loved the most, they have no trust in the Universe. It simply isn't safe to challenge the long-established beliefs. Because, in an effort to silence the abuse, they have silenced their inner voice and wisdom, they also tend to "drown out" anything good or positive.

Though Max seemed to "have it all" on the outside, he simply couldn't find joy in anything. Luckily, Max was willing to fight for freedom from this cycle. At the conclusion of our first session, Max was shocked to notice that he could hear out of his left ear! He reported to me the next week that the hearing seemed to be improving each day.

The Devastating Effects Of Sexual Trauma

In 1987, Penelope K. Trickett, a developmental psychologist, and Frank W. Putnam, a psychiatrist, collaborated on a study of the impact of interfamilial sexual abuse (incest) on female development [12]. This would be the first known study of its kind, following children who were victims of incest as they matured into adulthood. The focus of the study was to see how this kind of sexual abuse might influence them over time. Areas like performance in school, self-esteem, peer interactions/ relationships, and sexual activity were monitored.

The results of this, and numerous follow-up studies were clear. Trauma of this nature has a profound and lasting impact on nearly every area of these women's lives. Intellectual pursuits were impacted, with a significantly higher dropout rate. Psychologically, these individuals suffered from depression, self-mutilation, suicide, cognitive impairments, and other PTSD-related disorders. Physiologically, these women had increased disease, health conditions, obesity, and hormonal dysregulation. To make matters worse, research shows that sexual abuse in young women actually *speeds up* their body's sexual maturation by secreting sex hormones long before they would have naturally reached puberty [13].

As these young women were interviewed over time, the researchers found that this type of abuse continues to change their chemical physiology. While measuring hormone levels, the researchers realized that the women's bodies were chemically adjusting to *chronic trauma*. Over time, these women either learn to disassociate and "numb out" or become more erratic in their behavior [14].

It is abundantly clear that our childhood or even adult life can be dramatically altered by PNEs. In the next chapter, we will discuss some of our natural inclinations when we recognize trauma in our life.

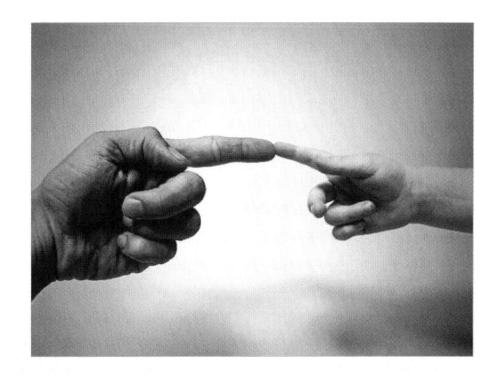

CHAPTER 7

So We Are All Traumatized... Who Is To Blame?

By now you are likely convinced of 3 things:

1. Trauma can have lasting negative effects on us, both consciously and subconsciously.

2. We all have experienced trauma of some form or another.

3. We probably shouldn't let it continue.

At least, I hope that is where you have landed. When most of us are faced with this knowledge, we often look for "who is to blame." As mentioned in Chapter 3, the lower model of the world, the Victim Model, is fixated on this question. We think that if we can identify the "WHO," we will figure out the "WHY" and all of our problems will be solved. One of the most likely recipients of this blame is our parents.

It's My Parents' Fault

In the late 1800s, Freud theorized that one of the main functions of psychoanalysis was to bring anger toward the parent into conscious awareness and that this would free the client from symptoms [1]. Unfortunately, this model of treatment has proven rather ineffective in actually resolving trauma. Well-meaning therapists may support or encourage an adult's anger at their parents for their parents' past behavior. This is based on an idea that a client will move away from self-blame if they get in touch with, and express that anger. And while validating feelings and perceptions *can* be a helpful or necessary early step in healing from a difficult childhood, this *continued* belief often leads to becoming trapped in old patterns and repeating hurtful relationship patterns.

Mind Change operates from the belief that "everyone is doing the BEST they can with what they have." Hopefully, from what you have learned thus far, you know that each of us has been undeniably shaped by various factors in our lives. Our parents are an incredibly significant factor. In fact, a popular theory of this impact is The Attachment Theory, originally developed by John Bowlby, a British psychoanalyst from the early 1900s. Bowlby was studying the behavior of infants who had been separated from their parents. Based on his findings, Bowlby theorized that infants who were able to maintain proximity to an attachment figure via attachment behaviors would be more likely to survive to a reproductive age [2].

Bowlby narrows this down to one question: "Is the attachment figure nearby, accessible, and attentive? If the child perceives the answer to this question to be "yes," he or she feels loved, secure, and confident, and, behaviorally, is likely to explore his or her environment, play with others, and be sociable. If, however, the child perceives the answer to this question to be "no," the child experiences anxiety and, behaviorally, is likely to exhibit attachment behaviors ranging from simple visual searching on the low extreme to active following and vocal signaling on the other. These behaviors continue until either the child is able to re-establish a desirable level of physical or psychological proximity to the attachment figure, or until the child "wears down," as may happen in the context of a prolonged separation or loss. In such cases, Bowlby believed that young children experienced profound despair and depression" (Bowlby, 1958).

Bowlby believed that attachment characterized human experience from "the cradle to the grave." [3] Many proponents of The Attachment Theory believe similarly to Bowlby, that if the model is formed early, it is stamped in as a template forever. Fortunately, the data doesn't support this. Even our DNA, thought to be set and unchangeable, can be changed (more on Epigenetics later).

Mind Change

But what we have to understand is that our parents can only give us what they personally have. What I mean is that most of our parents did not grow up with the most ideal circumstances either. Some came from broken homes, strict religious ideals, abuse, war-torn families, or emotionally unavailable caregivers. Yet, we expect that becoming a parent should somehow endow them with skills they were never given.

I grew up in a very unhealthy and codependent relationship with my own mother. Somewhere along the line, I had received (or perceived) the message that she *needed* me to help her. Fraught with alcoholism and drug use, my parents divorced when I was 4. Maybe because she was single or perhaps because she seemed emotionally fragile, I took it upon myself to become her "protector." Almost 40 years later, this seems like a preposterous idea. But to a scared and confused child, it made sense. My mother was my everything, and I needed for her to be safe. My mother was raised in a broken home, with a severely mentally unstable and alcoholic father. Addiction, physical abuse, and sexual abuse ran rampant in immediate and extended family. My mother's own painful past did not miraculously cease when she had children. If anything, it brought up painful insecurities and more opportunities to "fail." Her own addiction blossomed, and she turned to drugs, men, and work to silence her inner critic.

My own codependency took a turn when I left home at 11 years old. Trying to escape the turmoil of an abusive and addicted stepfather, I naively believed that if I left, she would follow. She didn't. This realization shook my identity and I quickly lost purpose. I moved from state to state, living with different family members, always hoping my mother would "choose me."

A couple of years later, she did eventually leave the abusive situation and we reunited under my grandmother's roof. By this time, I was bitter and resentful and became increasingly disapproving. Once the dutiful and committed daughter, I was now a strict "parole officer," keeping a rigid expectation of clean living. Of course, this only played into the already fragile dynamic that existed. My high school years were a painful time for us all. The mother/daughter role reversal that took place during that time was a comfortable misery.

Later in life, I used these and numerous other painful memories to develop my own sets of coping skills. As I shared before, these could not be silenced for long, and my declining health spoke the real story of the pain. One of my most profound tools for healing was the understanding that my parents were *doing the best they could with what they had been given*. When it became SO real to me that my mom loved me the best possible way she could at the time, it changed my perspective and ultimately, my life. Knowing some of her own traumatic past made it easy to see that she couldn't possibly give me things she didn't, herself, possess.

For the longest time, I had operated under the belief that rather than love me, she chose men, drugs, alcohol, or work. I honestly thought she had a choice and was choosing *them* over *me*. You might guess what kind of conclusions I made about myself at that point. I was forever trying to *earn* and *deserve* the love I could never seem to get from her. Why? What was wrong with me? Why wouldn't she love me? Rather than be angry at her, I kept trying to prove my value (ironically, by trying to "save" her from herself). Oh, how dysfunction gives birth to dysfunction!!

While doing my own Mind Change, it began to become clear to me that my mother actually loved me the best way she knew how. In fact, a large motivation for her continued self-medicating, was to cover up the guilt and shame she felt concerning her mothering abilities. Being a good mother was SO important to her. She didn't want me to end up like she did. But she only had the skills and experiences she had, and most of what she knew was pain/shame/blame. In the past, she had verbally blamed me for her addictions. It was her belief, and eventually, the belief of one of her former husbands that I was the reason she used. I was 6 months pregnant with my first child when I was blamed, solely, for her addiction. This caused the first of numerous estrangements.

Many years later, I revisited that statement and realized that for her, it was probably true. But not for the reasons I had initially thought. I realized that I represented, in living form, her failures as a mother. Interestingly enough, not because I *wasn't* "good," but because I *was* good. Whenever we were together, I would simultaneously make her proud and also ashamed. Proud of what I had become, and ashamed that it was "in spite" of her.

Though she has never really taken responsibility for the events of the past, I have finally forgiven her in a way I hadn't been able to before. For the first time ever, I *knew* that she loved me and had always wanted what was best for me. What mother doesn't? In the past, I would have said mine! But I now know that she really did the best she could. She wanted to do even better but didn't possess the skills. That is no reflection on her, it just is. How can I hold someone else responsible for doing the best they could? Would I have liked it to be different? In some ways, yes. But my forgiveness of her and ultimately myself, has allowed me to unlock years of happy memories that I had locked away with the good.

My mother has fought hard over the years, and with the help of many of the modalities that I mention in this book, she has even obtained long stretches of sobriety. She still is not able to engage in a healthy relationship with me (yet!), as I imagine much of her thoughts are projections of the past. But I am in a very contented place. Though we do not speak, I am able to respect her choices and know she is doing the best she can. I am free to let go of all the PNEs and to find only the good that remains. I am free now to see all the wonderful things I learned from her. All the ways that I am like her. I am able to tell my children about the brave and adventurous woman who raised me.

Whenever I go "gaga" over a sunset or rainbow, or make my kids come and look at the stars, I acknowledge her contribution to my life. I will continue to hold a space for her, as she heals in my own mind, hoping that someday it will be safe enough for her to come into the present and rewrite the past. I feel that I am loving her more now than I have ever been able to before. This is the gift that I am finally giving to myself.

CHAPTER 8

Dis-Ease: Language Of The Body

"This is the reason why the cure of so many diseases is unknown to the physicians of Hellas; they are ignorant of the whole. For this is the great error of our day in the treatment of the human body, that the physicians separate the mind from the body."

Socrates - "Plato's Charmides"

Before we dive into this subject, I want to remind you of a few things. In 1865, there was a Hungarian physician named Ignaz Philipp

Semmelweis. He was later committed to an insane asylum after a nervous breakdown. He had suffered great persecution from fellow doctors. Semmelweis was relentlessly mocked and ridiculed by his peers. Why? He had suggested that doctors should *wash their hands* after examining a patient. In those times, it was believed that a gentleman's hands were always clean. Doctors were gentlemen, so they did not need to wash their hands. At that time, doctors didn't wash their hands after examining a patient, before or after delivering a baby, or even after performing an autopsy. Bed linens were not washed, and surgical instruments were cleaned only when they were put away for storage [1]. This was just over 150 years ago.

Today, we are well aware that mercury is an extremely toxic and harmful environmental pollutant. In the sixteenth century, scientists and physicians used this "liquid silver" extensively in treating patients. They believed it to be a miraculous substance capable of eradicating most diseases. Even until the 1990s, mercuric compounds were an essential ingredient in drugs in both Asian and European countries. As a result, more people died of mercury poisoning than from the diseases they were actually suffering from [2].

In no way do I endeavor to detract from the amazing advancements in science and medicine. I have no formal medical training and do not intend to undermine the countless years of dedication and experience that medical professionals undertake. Given my propensity toward breaking bones, I am eternally grateful for the trained physicians whose care I have been in (more times than I would like to admit). That being said, we are in a global health crisis. And for the most part, physicians around the world are at a loss when it comes to reversing chronic illness.

The American Autoimmune Related Diseases Association (AARDA) estimates that up to 50 million Americans suffer from an autoimmune disorder [3]. This is up from 9 million in 1997—an *increase* of 41 million people in just over 20 years. The mortality rate due to Alzheimer's disease has increased by 123% from 2000 to 2015 [4]. Our world is getting sicker.

A study conducted by the Mayo Clinic shows:
- Almost 70% of Americans take at least one prescription
- Over 50% of Americans take two or more prescriptions
- 20% of Americans were found to be on 5 or more concurrent medications
- The top prescribed drugs in the United States are antibiotics, antidepressants, and painkilling opioids
- The second most common prescription is antidepressants [5]

But my guess is that these numbers don't surprise you. I think we are all aware of the prescription epidemic that we find ourselves in. Have you ever stopped to wonder why? Theories abound: GMOs, global warming, toxic environments, etc. While I wholeheartedly believe that our environment can influence our health, I have seen that our *emotional* environment is a far bigger influencer on health than our *physical* environment.

The Body Is The Mind

Hippocrates, a Greek physician who lived from about 460 B.C. to 375 B.C., is widely known as the "father of medicine." Almost 3,000 years later, medical doctors still hold his principles sacred: treat the sick to the best of one's ability, keep them from harm and injustice, preserve patient privacy, and teach the secrets of medicine to the next generation. Summing up the "Hippocratic Oath" that many medical school graduates still recite today, a famous quote by Hippocrates states, "*It is more important to know what sort of person has a disease than to know what sort of disease a person has.*" [6]

The idea that disease is more than a collection of symptoms has been around since the dawn of medicine. Though we have drastically strayed from this approach to health and wellbeing, I believe there is a reason that these great scholars started with the whole being.

Think for a minute about how we approach the diagnosis of illness or disease today. You have identified that there is something amiss in your health and well being, so you make an appointment with your health care practitioner. Upon arrival (even before you see the doctor), your vital signs are taken as an initial indicator of wellness. After that, a nurse will usually consult with you to collect your various complaints or symptoms. By the time you see the doctor, they already have a general idea of what might be wrong with you based on the data collected so far. So without even meeting you, a preliminary diagnosis is formed. Once the doctor arrives, you are asked about more symptoms, and then a physical exam is performed to confirm the symptoms and reveal any further information.

They will then consult their experience/training, a book, a chart, a colleague, or an online source, to determine what "dis-ease" or condition fits with the symptoms. After the diagnosis is made, treatment is generally recommended. This treatment is suggested, not based on the individual per se, but with the standard of practice for this particular ailment. These days, that usually involves a prescription of some sort. You are sent home with your new drug. Please come back if it doesn't work.

I would like to share an excerpt out of the University of California at San Diego's *Practical Guide to Clinical Medicine:*

History of Present Illness (HPI)

"Obtaining an accurate history is the critical first step in determining the etiology of a patient's problem. A large percentage of the time, you will actually be able to make a diagnosis based on the history alone. The value of the history, of course, will depend on your ability to elicit relevant information. Your sense of what constitutes important data will grow exponentially in the coming years as you gain a greater understanding of the pathophysiology of disease through increased exposure to patients and illness. However, you are already in possession of the tools that will enable you to obtain a good history. That is, an ability to listen and ask common-sense questions that help define the nature of a particular problem. It does not take a vast, sophisticated fund of knowledge to successfully interview a patient. In fact seasoned physicians often lose site of this important point, placing too much emphasis on the use of testing while failing to take the time to listen to their patients. Successful interviewing is for the most part dependent

upon your already well developed communication skills. What follows is a framework for approaching patient complaints in a problem oriented fashion. The patient initiates this process by describing a symptom. It falls to you to take that information and use it as a springboard for additional questioning that will help to identify the root cause of the problem. Note that this is different from trying to identify disease states which might exist yet do not generate overt symptoms." [7]

If only the medical students also saw this modeled rather than just mentioned. Notice it says, "Obtaining an accurate history is the critical first step in determining the etiology of a patient's problem." Oh, how deeply I agree with this!! Except our current medical world tends to focus on *medical* history rather than *personal* history. Listen, I totally get this. Doctors don't really have the time to go through all the components of a person's history, especially when our subconscious mind tends to be good at "storing away" the crucial details. But just because it doesn't happen, doesn't mean it shouldn't.

Nearly every culture since the beginning of time had identified our *mental* and emotional wellbeing as being directly linked to our *physical* wellbeing. The Bible is full of references showing the connection between mind and body. Proverbs 17:22 (NIV) says, *"A cheerful heart is good medicine, but a crushed spirit dries up the bones."*

Let's use a common example. The study done by the Mayo Clinic that I referenced above says that the 2nd most prescribed drug category is antidepressants. I have my own history with antidepressants. At age 16, after the urging of my mother, I went to the doctor to "diagnose" my depression. How did I know I was depressed? My mom told me. My mother, and most of the rest of her family, were on at least one antidepressant. "It runs in the family." This is what I heard and what I believed. So I assumed that I was, in fact, depressed and needed medication. I was diagnosed "Bi-polar" and "Manic Depressive" based on my symptoms. This was blamed on a "chemical imbalance" in my brain.

To be honest, I don't remember many details. But I do remember having blood taken, so I just assumed that they could detect this "imbalance" through my blood work. As I understood it, my body wasn't making enough "happy chemicals"; therefore, I was sad. I dutifully received my prescriptions. Zoloft was the first of many drugs I would take for my "dis-order." This started a nearly 10-year relationship with antidepressants. Take a Xanax if I got "too high" and the Zoloft (or a myriad of other choices) to keep me from going "too low."

Looking back, it was pretty easy to figure out why I was sad. Or mad. Or occasionally happy. My mother was battling addiction, and we had a tumultuous relationship at best. Two years prior, I had started high school in the small Nebraska town we had settled in. I was the "new kid," yet again, having attended 8 or more different schools in different states since starting 1st grade. High school brought its own set of challenges, including the onset of puberty wreaking havoc on my already fragile systems, and being surrounded by kids who had been together since kindergarten. Even some of their parents had gone to school together!

I was a new kid with a single mom who struggled with drug and alcohol addiction. We didn't have much money, and I didn't have great interpersonal skills! I did my best to fit in and make friends, but at the high price of trying to hide all of the drama at home. The pretending exacts a toll. The comparisons of my situation and the "normal families" was a constant burden. Watching my mother fight her personal demons and the development of my own was a daily battle. When my little brother got busted for selling weed while in middle school, I had even more ammunition to look down on myself and my perceived failures.

All of this was compounded by the slow and painful death of my beloved grandmother. My Grandma Pat was an incredible woman, and I felt unconditionally loved by her. She developed brain cancer, and within a year she was gone. Her wretched and speedy decline happened in our home. My mother, taking sole responsibility for her care. Given what you know of my situation at the time, you can imagine the impact that had on us all. My father had also remarried to a woman with 2 other children and an addiction problem herself. My stepmother was not a fan of me, and the feeling was mutual. They had another child when I was sixteen.

Between my hormones and my home life...is it any wonder I was "depressed"? The drugs only dimmed my already-challenged ability to "feel," keeping me in the foggy middle. Which, I suppose, seemed a superior option than feeling the real effects from the roller-coaster that my life was at the time. Looking back, I realize that I didn't "feel" very much during those years. Though from the outside I seemed fine—I got good grades and was popular enough—I was learning to "dull" my emotions rather than deal with them. It led to some strange and destructive behavior, particularly in the area of friendships. I was quick to burn bridges if people got "too close" and became callous if I really cared for someone because I feared the rejection of someone really knowing me.

Considering my own experience with "depression," I had a particular interest in finding out what really goes on with this condition. So let's look at some of the science.

How We "Do" Depression

First, I think it's important to understand that depression is something we "do," not something we "have." This is actually the case with most physical dis-eases. Your body and mind have to "do" quite a few things in order to produce what we now call depression. Contrary to what I believed, depression was NOT *caused* by a chemical imbalance in my brain. Rather, depression was a *result* of what I *did* in my brain. For my body to produce any symptoms of "depression," I first had to create it in my brain.

Increasingly sophisticated forms of brain imaging technologies permit a much closer look at the working brain than was possible in the past. The use of these various scans has led to a better understanding of which brain regions regulate mood and how other functions, such as memory, may affect depression. The parts of the brain that play a major role in depression are the hippocampus, amygdala, and the thalamus. How interesting! Are these not the same areas involved in the creation and storage of memories? So doesn't it seem logical that our memories and what we have stored within them could be a contributing factor to depression?

Dis-Ease: Language of the Body

In the past, researchers believed that depression resulted in a low production of neurotransmitters. We have chemicals in our brain that carry messages between neurons. These chemicals are called Neurotransmitters. Antidepressant medications often increase these chemicals. If depression is a result of low neurotransmitter quantity, then people should feel better as soon as levels of neurotransmitters increases, right? But that is not the case. It usually takes days or even weeks for someone to see the effects. The top neurotransmitters that are believed to play a role in depression are:

- Acetylcholine
- Serotonin
- Norepinephrine
- Dopamine
- Glutamate

These chemicals help regulate our moods but are also created by our feelings and emotions. Stress also creates chemicals, like cortisol. Remember, stress is an automatic response to any stimuli that requires us to adjust or change. Threats, real or perceived, will trigger a flood of stress hormones to the body. These hormones produce physiological changes within the body. Bruno Dubuc of the Douglas Hospital Research Centre in Quebec, Canada says, "Prolonged chronic stress also seems to alter the response of the MR and GR receptors and to have very harmful effects on people's mental equilibrium, especially when social or family supports are absent. Under these conditions, the glucocorticoid response, which was originally highly adaptive, becomes clearly maladaptive." [8]

Basically, this means that stressful events, or PNEs as we call them, actually alter the way our brain produces and regulates the "feelings" chemicals in our brain. If we continue to rehearse (subconsciously) negative experiences or painful past memories, we produce chemicals in alignment with those negative experiences. Excess cortisol and other "stress hormones" produced over a prolonged time will inhibit or "depress" the production of other "feel good" chemicals. In essence, you are chemically *practicing* producing stress hormones. So eventually, the brain produces less and less "feel good" chemicals. The end result being...you feel pretty darn "depressed."

Depression is real. Because the feelings are real. Chemically, your body is over-producing chemicals that feel bad. It's pretty difficult to feel good when you feel so bad. So what's the answer? Well, once again, we need to address the root cause. If the root cause of the negative feelings is the stress hormones, then it stands to reason that we would look at the *cause* of the stress hormones. If the cause of the stress hormone production is the myriad of painful memories that populate the "filing system," then doesn't it make sense to address the memories?

But we have settled for a synthetic approach. Rather than deal with the "how" my body keeps producing these negative chemicals, we take a pill that has synthetic "happy" in it. Here is the problem..."synthetic happy" never lasts. We will always need more because our chemicals will still be at war. Your body continues to produce cortisol and other stress hormones in an attempt to communicate with you and keep you safe ("Hey! There is some really NOT GOOD stuff you keep thinking and remembering and it's scaring the crap out of us.").

What do you think would happen if the filing system were full of good, happy memories? What chemicals would your body produce? If your mind sorted through your files and found safety, security, and love, what hormones would have to be created to support those feelings? Definitely not stress hormones!! What if, every day, you woke up and remembered all the good things that happened to you? If you were filled with gratitude and contentment. After some time, your body would get really good at producing serotonin (regulates sleep, appetite, and mood, and inhibits pain), dopamine (pleasure hormone: influences motivation and plays a role in how a person perceives reality), and Gamma-Aminobutyric Acid, or GABA (inhibits fear, helps quell anxiety). This may even suppress the body's ability to produce cortisol or norepinephrine (constricts blood vessels, raises blood pressure, triggers anxiety).

If your brain were producing the "feel-good hormones" in abundance, how do you think you would wake up each day? Pretty darn good! You wouldn't even have to try, it just would be! Once I began addressing my PNEs and re-populating my files with good memories, I no longer *did* depression. I began to *do* a lot of happiness and hopefulness. I used to believe that I could only regulate my moods with a pill or a mixture of pills. I know differently now. If I ever begin to "feel" depressing feelings, I realize that I must be thinking depressing thoughts. I am literally "depressing" my feel-good chemicals.

My "prescription" for depressing feelings looks very different now. Now, I know that I need to take some time for myself. Invest in ME! Spend some time doing things that make me feel good. I regulate my moods now. Truth is, I always did, but I wasn't always aware of it. Now that I am, I am intentional about it. I take care of myself, even down to my chemical creations in my body!

Yeah, But...*My* Disease Is Real

I believe every dis-ease is real because I believe that "thoughts become things." I **know** how powerful our minds are. I know that we can create and produce incredible and fearful things in our bodies, just with our thoughts. So, I know what comes next...

"I have _____ (fill in the blank: Lyme, cancer, MCS, MS, etc.). Are you saying I actually *created* this in my body?"

Yes and No. If this "triggers" you in any way, go take a walk and a few deep breaths and come back. You won't want to miss this next part (though you may not like it...at first).

Remember a fundamental, irrevocable truth: *The body can do NOTHING without the permission of the mind.* Nothing. We know this. When it comes to basic functions, we know this to be true. But when it comes to dis-ease, physical or mental illness, we balk. Why?

This goes back to Chapter 3 and the Victim Model of the world. As humans, we almost always demand a "Why." And more importantly, "who is to blame." Without a reason or an outside force to blame, we flail about, trying to find an answer that somehow doesn't place us in the crosshairs of responsibility. The keyword to this is "blame." If you are to blame for your illness, that is almost always "bad." In that sense, I would rarely say that someone is to *blame* for their condition. But I do believe we are *responsible*. Social psychologist, Dr. Amy Johnson, states the following on her blog:

"Responsibility is empowering. It's powerful. It's all good. When you take responsibility for your life, you put yourself in the

driver's seat.   When you take responsibility for having hurt someone, you accept what you did so that you can learn from your mistakes and move on. Responsibility = Acceptance. No wonder it feels so good to finally take responsibility after having shirked it. Blame, on the other hand, is disempowering.   When you blame yourself for the state of your life, you're telling yourself the lie that you aren't in charge. You become a victim.   When you blame yourself for having hurt someone else, you just feel shame and shame has no upside." [9]

Think of your mind and body as a garden.   The mind is the soil. Memories are seeds. If you look around your garden and see only weeds, it would be a good idea to look at what you have planted.   If you have planted weeds and thorns and thistles, don't be surprised if that is what grows.   To have a thriving garden that will nourish you, you need first to plant the seeds of the plants you would like to harvest.   Because you weren't the only one planting seeds in the early years, you are welcome to observe your garden and only keep the plants that you choose.   Better yet, you can also plant a wonderful array of seeds that will produce a plentiful harvest over time.

So back to physical illness...let me ask you a question.   Have you ever noticed how a flu bug goes around, and some people get it and some people don't?   Why is that?   Especially within a family.   I don't know about you, but I can put myself in a sterile bubble, and my children will still "share" germs with me!   They can't share toys...but germs?   No problem. I remember a story of a friend who traveled abroad as a teenager with a large group of other people.   They had all taken anti-malaria tablets

120

before the trip. But still, a couple of the kids and one or two adults came down with it. Why?

In an attempt to explain this phenomenon, scientists have theorized various possibilities. Let's take the common cold. Dr. Ellen Foxman, a professor at Yale School of Medicine, explains, "The airway does pretty well if it encounters one stressor at a time. But when there are two different stressors, there's a trade-off. What we found is that when your airway is trying to deal with another stress type, it can adapt, but the cost is susceptibility to rhinovirus infection." [10]

The "stress" that Dr. Foxman is suggesting are *environmental* stressors like pollen, cigarette smoke, viruses, etc. But let's examine the next conclusion Dr. Foxman arrives at. "Research has found that cigarette smokers tend to be more susceptible to rhinovirus infection compared to people who don't smoke" (Foxman, 2015). Interesting. It's very easy to correlate the ill effects of smoking with an increased risk of rhinovirus, but what if we took that even further. Why are they smoking in the first place?

Helptoquit.com says, "Some people might smoke because it feels like it helps them cope with negative feelings and emotions, leaving them with a heightened sense of wellbeing. Some people with mental health problems, such as depression or anxiety, might smoke because it helps to alleviate some of the symptoms they experience. Either way, they feel like smoking keeps their emotions under control, helping them to cope."

What if it's actually the stress that's the problem? Stephen Linsteadt, NHD, CNC, co-founder of Natural Healing House and coauthor of *The Heart of Health: the Principles of Physical Health and Vitality* says,

> *"A disruption in our consciousness can create an area of stagnation or incoherence in our bodies that can derail DNA transcription, suppress T-cell and NK-cell activity and other immune system functions, and lead to chronic and degenerative illnesses, depression, and other psychosis."* [11]

We've already established that PNEs (perceived negative experiences) can have a very real effect on the way our body produces chemicals, perceives safety and danger, and regulates our responses and behaviors. Any "mis-fire" or "mis-wire" of these systems with hormones, immune cells, and organs, contributes to disease and poor health. Modern science now confirms that negative emotions can make you ill. Unfortunately, exactly when and how one becomes ill as a result of negative emotions cannot be accurately charted. The extent of the damage of an emotion or stressful event may take years to develop into a condition like cancer, or may erupt immediately in an attack of shingles or an outbreak of cold sores.

In a study by the *American Psychological Association*, 217 people were questioned about their work, and how stressed they were. Their saliva samples were also taken. Results found that those who exhibited low self-esteem or self-blame tended to have less immunoglobulin-A, making them more susceptible to respiratory infections [12]. In a separate study published in the *Proceedings of the National Academy of Sciences*, 270 participants were told to think of an event that made them feel either happy or sad. Then, they were given a flu vaccine and monitored for six months. Participants who exhibited better immunity—and more antibodies in their blood—were those with the strongest activity in their prefrontal cortex, associated with positive thoughts [13].

When something is "off" in our subconscious mind, frequently an incongruency caused by PNEs in our past, the body is the place where that problem plays out. Often, illness or dis-ease in our bodies is representative of what is happening in our mind. They are "final warning signs" in the communication system between mind and body.

Pain Is Communication?

This isn't something you are going to hear in mainstream media or even in the office of your primary care physician. We, as a society, are deeply entrenched in the way we do "health care." The pharmaceutical companies are quite happy with the direction we have been going. It lines their pockets but keeps people sicker than ever. Rather than make a political statement here, I want to focus on the positive reality of this situation. Our health is in our hands.

Though you probably haven't heard anything about the degree to which our emotional and thought life affects our physical health, that doesn't mean that the information hasn't been there. For centuries, even back to the time of Hippocrates, people were aware of this connection. In the Bible, Proverbs 23:7 is often quoted as saying, "As a man thinks, so he shall be..."

Dis-Ease: Language of the Body

Louise Hay published her first book *Heal Your Body*, in 1976. She was instrumental in not only illustrating the mind/body connection but also in connecting various limiting beliefs to specific ailments or diseases in the body. She wasn't the first to do so, but is arguably the most well known. Inna Segal, the author of *The Secret Language of Your Body*, is another individual who linked specific illnesses to life events or negative feelings/ emotions.   These authors were instrumental in my own journey to wellness. Being someone who wasn't particularly skilled at "feeling my feelings," their texts became a reference system for what was going on with me emotionally.

For instance, I had long suffered from pain in my lower back. Though I had seen countless doctors, tried various forms of treatments from steroid injections/painkillers/muscle relaxers to yoga and pilates, nothing seemed to work. I was told genetics were at play as well as lifestyle. Being a horse trainer in my earlier years and suffering numerous falls definitely provided an easy explanation of why my back always seemed to hurt. Interestingly enough, it didn't always hurt the same way. Sometimes I could barely feel it, and other times I was lying on a hospital gurney writhing in pain despite every available painkiller. If it actually was something physical, why did the symptoms change so drastically?

It wasn't until I began addressing my past physical abuse that I saw the first real relief in the pain. Louise Hay, in *You Can Heal Your Life*, says that back pain is about support. Specifically, lower back pain can indicate "fear of money and lack of financial support." [14] That definitely could fit, but when I referenced Inna Segal's book *The Secret Language of Your Body*, she had this to say about the pain: "Feeling unsupported and alone.

124

Not knowing who or where to ask for help. Feeling that the world is an unsafe place to live in. Trying to protect yourself from pain and hurt..." [15] That definitely resonated with me! Her book even broke it down further into the different vertebrae. I knew that I had been diagnosed with herniations in the L4 and L5 regions, so I looked those up. In the L5 description, it said "Holding on to feelings of betrayal, abandonment, and isolation. Difficulty trusting people and following through with plans. Frequent self-sabotage, anger, and anxiety. A tendency to see yourself as a victim..." (Segal, 2007) BINGO!!

These insights allowed me to "hone in" on some of the problem areas in my life. Obviously, I was quickly transported back to the first time I felt or believed these things and found myself back in my childhood. I thought that my back was the problem. I had MRIs and scans to show the "damage," but I just wanted to feel better. My spine surgeon (who had previously operated on my neck and fused 2 of my vertebrae...another story!) said something to me during the discussions of yet another surgery on my spine. When discussing my particular herniations, I asked why it hurt so badly. He said that they didn't actually know. He said that so much of what happens with the spine is still a mystery. He said that he has scanned thousands of spines over the years. He had seen people with much worse herniations than mine who felt no pain whatsoever and some with even smaller ones who were in constant, unbearable pain.

This very well-respected and educated surgeon told me that they actually have no idea what the connection is. He said that they often do surgery just hoping to alleviate some pain, but that the outcomes are unreliable at best. This information caused me to pause and think. What if the pain had little to nothing to do with what the scans showed...but something else altogether? It wasn't until I found myself down the "rabbit hole" of my own mind/body healing journey that his words came back to me. What if the pain had a message for me?

Though Inna Segal and Louise Hay were pivotal in my journey of communicating with my body, I eventually moved to even more in-depth resources. I was shocked to find many resources that go into incredible detail about the "emotional drivers" behind dis-ease and illness. Over the years, these have become invaluable tools as I explore the body messages to myself and my clients.

I have come to see illness, disease, syndromes, and ailments as communication. I no longer think, "What did I eat?" "What might I have?" "Maybe I should go see a doctor." My first reaction is to find out what my mind is trying to communicate to me through my body. I am particularly skilled in having my body deliver messages to me. I believe this is something I developed over time because I was not well versed in "feeling emotions." I beat myself up over this for many years as an adult. I had interacted with enough people at this point to realize that I wasn't a very "emotional" person. It seemed that I had two main emotions—"mad" or "fine." That was about it. I didn't get "hurt," I got mad. From someone who was formerly diagnosed bi-polar, this might seem like a good happy medium! But it didn't really serve me, especially because I had children.

Interestingly enough, though I had multiple physical issues before, the conception and birth of my children were a huge catalyst in the downfall of my health. I know now that the emotional components to that were my stressed relationship with my own mother and my fears of being a parent. All I knew were my own parents and the way I felt about growing up. I didn't feel that I possessed any skills to do it differently, and it wreaked havoc on my body. My body was screaming out to deal with these things, but because I didn't know how to listen, I continued to worsen over time.

I was speaking to a friend prior to embarking on the mind/body journey about my "inability to feel." He also happened to be a therapist. He was aware of my tumultuous upbringing and reframed this for me in a beautiful way. "Thank God you didn't *feel* much as a kid. What a gift! Can you imagine what your life would have been like if you had *felt* every bad thing that had happened to you and you were aware of it? Your mind was protecting you. What a wonderful skill it provided you with. The problem is, though it kept you alive and sane as a child, it no longer serves you as an adult."

YES!! That was it. In that moment, rather than beat myself up for "not feeling," I loved myself for taking such good care of me. Luckily, this was right before I began finding the answers to how to actually change those programs. Even if they once kept me safe.

Someone might say, "Okay, I could see how some autoimmune *syndrome* might be associated with feelings, but what about a broken arm? Huh? That surely can't be emotional. Am I supposed to just *feel* the bone back together?" Do you get the feeling I have been asked this before?

Here is what I have to say about that. First of all, I have fallen off of horses more times than I can count. And though I have broken many bones, I don't always break something when I fall. Is it just the way I fall? Maybe. But there is also an insight into what seems like random events.

Which arm did I break? The right? The left? Questions such as these hold possible clues to a message from the mind. *Is it possible that I have been feeling something that I haven't been dealing with? Am I having to reevaluate my usual way of doing things, because my way is no longer effective?*

Knowing this will not "un-break" my arm.   But it can aid in the healing. It can also fortify areas of your life or belief systems that might be weak so that your arms are strengthened.

I want to share a case study that will hopefully help illustrate this further.

MARTHA

Martha came to see me because she had been suffering from Chronic Lyme disease. She had done all of the protocols and had only gotten worse. After hearing about my story of overcoming Lyme and many other rare conditions, she decided to reach out. As always, I received a detailed history of PNEs. A few things caught my eye, one being that she was the oldest of multiple siblings raised by a single mother. And the second being that one of the siblings was disabled. Martha was too unwell to meet physically, so we agreed to meet online. Even over Skype, I noticed that Martha didn't look that sick.   Other than looking a little tired, she presented as a rather "put together" individual. As we began to work, a fuller picture began to emerge. She was the mother of two young children, ages 4 and 6. Her husband was loving and supportive and had become the primary caretaker of both Martha and her children. This was a source of shame for Martha.   She had been the Director of Operations at a halfway house for homeless girls. She loved her job and was very good at what she did, but had become too sick to continue. It quickly became clear that Martha was very hard on herself. She felt an enormous amount of guilt and shame about her illness but felt little hope about getting better. A common emotional connection with Lyme disease is a lack of personal boundaries. As a child, she was often responsible for the care of her siblings in her mother's absence. Her mother was a nurse at a local hospital and she was frequently absent. Martha had two younger siblings and the middle sibling suffered from Cerebral Palsy. Martha expressed her fears as a child that her brother might die in her care. Though his Cerebral Palsy was well managed, it was still a huge responsibility for such a young child. This was compounded by the importance she put on her mother's job. Likely to assuage her own guilt, her mother would often speak about the importance of her job at the hospital, sharing that the reason she was so needed at the hospital was that lives were at stake. Martha was confused by her feelings as a child. On the one hand, she felt proud of her mother for saving people's lives. On the other hand, she wished that her mother would spend more time taking care of her and her siblings. She remembered feeling ashamed that she needed her mother and had tried hard never to complain about the burden she felt at home. Martha often received praise from her mother and other adults for "how responsible" she was and how hard she worked. She rarely had time to think about her own needs and viewed friends at school as immature and having trivial problems. Even when her mother started showing the signs of substance abuse, Martha made excuses for her and rationalized her behavior. The only times that Martha received any real care and attention were the few times she had become sick. When a case of the measles took her out for almost two weeks, her mother was completely transformed into the doting caretaker. Martha reveled in the rare attention and reluctantly admitted to me that it was one of her favorite memories. It didn't take long to see what her body was trying to say with the Lyme disease. Her childhood conditioned her to look for approval in her hard work and care for others. Unfortunately, this was at the expense of her own needs. She felt immense gratification when she worked hard and "helped others," but the carefully crafted illusion would often wear thin, and she would resort to illness to "take a break" from the constant meeting of needs. When she had children, even her ever-increasing "sick days" didn't allow her the break that she desperately needed. The former attention that her husband would give her when she would get sick was now focused on the children, who seemed to still need her even if she was sick. Eventually, there were more sick days than well days, and a friend suggested she get tested for Lyme disease. Her mind's continued but unanswered plea for love and attention resulted in the message showing up in her body. Within a few sessions, Martha was able to acknowledge the pressure she felt as a child. We were able to go back and rewrite these memories. In allowing the feelings of hurt and abandonment to show up in a safe place, she was able to let them go. When she did this, Martha was able to clearly see all the ways she had received love and attention in a healthy way and came to see that her own mother had been doing the best she could at the time. Martha also realized that her fear of something happening to her little brother, who had Cerebral Palsy, had become so big that it has altered her perception of reality. In fact, her little brother actually had a rather mild case of Cerebral Palsy and had been a joy to be around. Her perception of the burden and responsibility had shaped her memory to see her brother as a fragile and helpless individual. Now, as she became free of the beliefs that she used to keep her safe as a child, she could clearly see how strong and successful her brother was. Rather quickly, Martha began to feel better. She began taking time for herself and used this as opportunity to love herself more genuinely. Her personal boundaries were strengthened, and she began to see her worth and value as something that just "was" rather than something she had to work for. Martha began to understand that her main "responsibility" was to continue to clean up her head. Keeping only the memories and experiences that served her and reframing or rewriting the rest. Not only did her Lyme disease resolve, but she began experiencing her children in a deeper way. Her relationship with her family improved, and she eventually returned back to work at the halfway house. Now, her main goal was to provide the girls in the program with the emotional tools to address the destructive thoughts, memories, patterns, and beliefs in their lives. She now views any incongruency in her physical health as a loving message from her mind. Now, Martha listens.

Stories like Martha's and my own are not uncommon. Over and over, I have seen illness and dis-ease be resolved by dealing with the PNEs in our lives. In the next chapter, I'll address some of the most common fears and concerns that people have with this kind of work.

> *"What happens in the mind of man is always reflected in the*
> *disease of his body."*
> Rene Dubos, (1901-1982)

CHAPTER 9

The Problem With Pain

In the next part of the book, I will begin to give you practicals for moving from the Victim Model of thinking to the Victor Model. But first, I believe it is important to explain what our *real* problem is...pain. Most of us will do nearly anything to avoid pain. Whether it's emotional, mental, or spiritual, pain is universally known as an unpleasant emotion. I don't necessarily believe that pain is the problem. Pain is often a valuable form of feedback. I think that it would be beneficial to understand a little more about what we call "pain."

Pain has been confounding experts since the Dawn of Man. Early philosophers like Plato and Aristotle reasoned that pain was simply an emotion, having no physiological root [1]. Alternatively, Hippocrates believed that pain was a result of imbalanced *fluids* within the body. None implicated the *brain* in the process, but rather the *heart* as the birthplace of pain [2].

Prior to the scientific Renaissance in Europe, it was still theorized that pain existed outside of the body. Religious sects believed pain was a punishment from God. The only treatment being prayer [3]. In other Christian teachings, pain was explained as a test or trial for a believer, inflicted by God to affirm their faith during trial-through-suffering. Once again, believing the source of pain was *outside* of the individual.

In 1664, French scientist and philosopher René Descartes theorized that pain was a signal passed down nerve fibers to the brain [4]. This theory transferred the cause of pain from something spiritual or mystical into something physical and mechanical. This also moved the responsibility of pain from the heart to the brain. Descartes' theory promoted something that is still believed today—that we have "pain nerves." Many people, including health care professionals, still believe that messages sent to the brain by these "pain nerves" will always cause pain because the *signal is pain*. Also, wrongly labeled "pain fibers" suggest that their messages will always send messages of pain.

Research now shows that no nerve we have is a "pain" nerve. No particular nerve can detect "pain." Nerves detect *stimulus* [5]. Our brain is the ultimate authority on defining the stimulus. Meaning, how we feel about it and what to do about it, if anything. Janet Bultitude, Lecturer in

Cognitive and Experimental Psychology at the University of Bath, explains it this way:

"Scientists distinguish between nociception – the nervous signal of damage to our body – and pain, the unpleasant emotional and cognitive experience that normally results when our nociceptors are activated. This means that pain is more than just a sensory experience, it is influenced by our thoughts, feelings and social relationships. For example, how we experience pain is affected by our thoughts, such as what we believe the pain might mean, and what we remember of previous painful experiences." [6]

In 2000, I experienced a fall through a window. The story is mildly entertaining, but I'll save it for another time. It resulted in a pretty beat up face (leaving a scar through my eyebrow), a broken finger, a "frozen" shoulder, and a neck injury that was first thought to be a fracture but luckily turned out otherwise. After many months of physical therapy, I was still experiencing terrible pain radiating from my neck down my right arm. I eventually had a "nerve conduction study" done to detect any possible nerve damage. With tiny little electrodes taped to various parts of my neck, hands, and arms, they sent little electrical currents through my body. Like most tests that have been performed on me over my lifetime, I wasn't entirely sure what they were looking for.

The results came back...nerve damage. A certain percentage of "nerve damage" was diagnosed and *voila*, I had my "answer" to my pain. The damage was said to be permanent, and I was told I would likely have some residual pain and numbness for the rest of my life. So what? Was my diagnosis a rare exception to what I mentioned above? No. Let me explain.

Nociceptive Vs. Neuropathic Pain

Allow me some technical phrasing for a moment. Remember that I mentioned that there are technically no "pain nerves"? That is true. But the nerves that are primarily associated with carrying the *stimuli* that the brain can choose to perceive as pain are called "nociceptors." If the brain chooses that "pain" is warranted, doctors call this pain "nociceptive pain." So if you decide to take the cake you are baking out of the oven with your bare hands, your nociceptors will carry *stimuli* (not pain, stimuli) to your brain. Your subconscious mind will accurately determine that not taking things out of the oven barehanded is a great skill to have, and will assist the building of this skill by giving you a strong incentive to NEVER try this again. That incentive, or message, will be carried back to your hand by the same nociceptors and you will feel OUCH!! Nociceptive pain should resolve as the body part heals.

Medical News Today says, "Neuropathic pain is a medical term used to describe the pain that develops when the nervous system is damaged or not working properly due to disease or injury." [7] Basically, doctors differentiate these two types of pain like this:

1. Nociceptive pain: "We've x-rayed your foot, and it is broken. That is why it hurts. It should start to feel better as it begins to heal."

2. Neuropathic pain: "Well, Mr. Smith, I know you say your back is hurting, but all the scans came back clear. It's likely a pinched nerve. It may or may not get better."

Chronic pain is usually categorized as neuropathic pain. It is different because it does not seem to develop as a result of any specific known circumstance or outside stimulus. It's also fascinating to know that people can suffer from neuropathic pain even when the affected body part is *not actually there*. It is estimated that nearly half of the people who have lost a limb have experienced feeling pain in the limb that they no longer have [8]. This condition is known as Phantom Limb Pain. At times, the pain can become debilitating.

Chronic low back pain is easily one of the most common complaints that people seek medical attention for, but in 90 percent of cases, doctors are not able to identify a physical cause [9]. Interesting. So, did I have "nerve damage"? Well, the pain increased over the years, leading me eventually to have spinal fusion on two of my cervical vertebra. Though, at the time, I felt like the pain had reduced after the surgery, it would still come back once in a while. It was only after I began dealing with the beliefs, negative thoughts, and painful memories from my past that I found permanent relief. So what does that have to do with nerves? Nothing.

So what is the problem with pain? Nothing. Pain is communication. It's your brain's way of telling you that something is "less than wonderful." Whether you are touching a hot stove or believing that you will never be "good enough," both of these *stimuli* will require a decision on the part of your brain. Pain is one of the preferred options to GET

YOUR ATTENTION! We are learning machines. Our subconscious mind is always gathering and sorting information to protect us and to help us adapt better to our environment. Not touching hot stoves is a crucial skill to learn. So is believing in yourself.

We seem hell-bent on not feeling pain of any sort. Physical pain *and* emotional pain are both creations of the mind. And they are done for our good. Take people who cannot feel pain. People who suffer from the condition Congenital Insensitivity to Pain (CIP), also known as congenital analgesia, are said to be unable to feel pain [10]. They have never felt pain. For many people, this seems like a wonderful ability. Not so. Normally associated with a gene mutation, these individuals often die in childhood due to the lack of communication between the mind and the body. They are unable to detect fractures, burns, or illness. In some cases, the body can *feel* or perceive damage, but they lack the proper ability to react. For instance, they can *feel* the pain of their hand burning on the hot stove but lack the proper communication between body and mind to remove the hand. Others, it seems, cannot even detect painful stimuli, essentially *unable* to feel anything resembling pain or discomfort.

Though we can all probably agree that this isn't exactly an ideal evolutionary development for physical pain, humankind still seems determined to try to accomplish this emotionally. Even the old playground battle cry of *"sticks and stones may break my bones but words can never hurt me"* speaks to our emotional fragility; otherwise, why would we try to drill this into our heads? The fact of the matter is that words do hurt. I've heard it said by many abuse victims that the worse abuse they suffered was verbal or emotional rather than physical. That resonates with my own abuse story. I remember a defining moment as a 10-year-old girl when I became aware that I couldn't *feel* my stepfather's blows any longer. I felt triumphant. I actually remember thinking that, since I could no longer feel it, I should now be the sole bearer of the abuse. I truly believed that I could protect my mother and little brother by attracting and enduring the physical ire of my stepfather because I was now immune to feeling it. I would later realize that the emotional pain of the abuse was far greater than the physical, and much longer-lasting.

What is my point? We so desperately want a way out of our pain. And we want to know WHY. Why does my back hurt? Why do I have fibromyalgia? Why do I have panic attacks? Why, why, why? But we want the answer to be physical. I can't tell you how many times I have heard this sentence... "Yes, I've been diagnosed with _____ (fill in the blank with any terrible diagnosis), BUT I'm just so happy to finally know what's wrong with me." We want answers. Under the guise that we will also find solutions. But what if there is nothing actually *wrong* with our body? What if we have just become really rotten at our communication?

Pain is communication. When we listen, it often goes away. What if your lower back is trying to tell you that you deeply lack self-worth and often don't possess the boundaries to say "no." Or the belief that you have to work harder than others to be accepted. Things seem to come easy to others but you have to work harder than other people do. What if your lower back, the leverage point of your entire self, is screaming out to let go of the heavy burden you've been carrying for all these years. Do you need a surgery? Only if it involves the precise removal of all of the beliefs keeping you in alignment with the pain you hold. Do you need a pain pill? Only if you want to temporarily dull your ability to *feel* anything.

I took something very valuable from learning about the way our body processes stimuli. The circular nature of it. If pain is, simply put, the communication decision that comes from the brain after receiving the information from the source, what would happen if that message was intercepted? Remember, I previously mentioned the "Telephone Game"? A message is sent from the first person through many other people to eventually get back to the originator of the message. This concept gives us a big tool in our healing process. I will go into this in much more detail in Chapter 16.

The actual experience of pain is in the head, not in the body. And, surprisingly, this is true of all forms of pain. Someone can have an injury without having pain. I have heard numerous stories from the battlefields of war. One such story told of a man who had been involved in a landmine explosion. After it happened, the man realized that many of his fellow soldiers were grievously injured. He began helping as many as possible to safety. It wasn't until the medics arrived that he suspected something was amiss. Instead of attending to the hurt men around him, the man found himself being laid upon a stretcher. He had half of his head blown off and you could clearly see part of his brain from the gaping hole. The man hadn't been aware he was even injured and reported no pain until realizing the gravity of his own condition.

Pain can also occur *without* an actual physical injury. In 1995, the British Medical Journal reported a case of a construction worker who had jumped off of scaffolding and had apparently been impaled through the foot by a large nail that went through his steel-toed boot. The man arrived at the hospital in tremendous pain, and doctors debated on how to remove the nail. With the boot still on, even the slightest movement of the nail caused excruciating pain and he was given powerful painkillers and sedatives. When the boot was finally removed, however, the nail had not actually punctured the foot at all. It had lodged between his toes, missing the foot entirely [11].

Knowing that all pain is generated in our minds is a powerful tool in the Mind Change process. This information will be critical when we move into the practicals of the Mind Change Method.

CHAPTER 10

Will This Work For Me?

Change will not come if we wait for some other person or some other time. We are the ones we've been waiting for. We are the change that we seek.

Barack Obama

The most difficult thing is the decision to act, the rest is merely tenacity. The fears are paper tigers. You can do anything you decide to do. You can act to change and control your life; and the procedure, the process is its own reward.

Amelia Earhart

141

People ask me what kinds of people this works for and I usually say that it works for people who have problems. When they ask what kind of problems, I usually respond with, "Any problem you can *think* of." I sometimes add that it helps if they have a brain....since that is what we will be working with! But most of the people I work with have a very good reason for asking. They have "tried everything" and are still just as bad, if not worse. Why?

It's not because they don't want it. It's not because they haven't tried. It's not because they aren't "good enough," "smart enough," or "strong enough." It's because they know *HOW* to put all of their hope, money, and energy into something and have it "fail." They weren't consciously trying to fail. In fact, according to the subconscious mind...they succeeded. They succeeded in keeping things just the way they are because often, it's not safe to change.

Secondary Gains

As I mentioned before, if we are doing something, we likely have a very good reason for it. Otherwise, we wouldn't be doing it. A problem isn't a failure, it's a success. You aren't "failing at being healthy," you are successful at being sick! If you stopped being successful, you would fail to be sick. Clear as mud?

Here's the deal...we need to start seeing our lives as a success. I am successful at not losing weight. I am successful at producing this cancer. I am successful at sabotaging good opportunities in my life. The reason is, if I can be successful at some things, it presupposes that I can be

142

successful at something else. A problem is just an undesired success. So we can choose to be successful at something else! But often, we see something as a problem but neglect to acknowledge the benefits we get from it. When we benefit from something that, on the surface, looks negative; we call that Secondary Gains.

If I'm overweight, someone will finally love me for who I am and not what I look like. If I self-sabotage good job opportunities, I won't ever have to face the pressure that comes with maintaining success. If I am sick, I won't be expected to do all those things that drain me emotionally. And so on...

It may not be easy to identify the Secondary Gains in our lives. Our subconscious mind keeps these safely guarded. We are often reluctant to give up certain undesirable outcomes if there are "good things" that come from it, especially if the subconscious mind has used this to "keep you safe." Remember the statistics regarding obesity and sexual abuse? Weight gain is often a metaphoric "barrier" of protection. Almost like emotional padding. It's also a deterrent from unwanted sexual attention. Note that these are conclusions made by the subconscious since we are not often consciously aware.

So when a client comes into sessions with some of the following programs, I know that these are just safety mechanisms and patterns of thinking that have been practiced. Sometimes, the first number of sessions deal specifically with these patterns. Here are some:

"I've tried everything. Nothing works for me."

This program comes from a file folder that has many "proofs" or "references" that this is true. This is often an indicator that there may be Secondary Gains to the problem. We will normally need to address the "what if's" behind them getting better. A common fear associated with this is, "Who will I be if I don't have this problem?" To deal with this, we will often need to go back and find out why it's so important that it *doesn't* work. People are often flustered by this, being completely ignorant to the "good" that the subconscious mind is trying to protect.

"Yes, but my disease/illness/diagnosis is REAL. I have proof!"

Again, I will say that YES, your issue is real. To you. I know that you feel it or can see it. You likely have some sort of diagnostic proof to back up your reality. This was the case for me. I had a medical file the size of three stacked encyclopedias. I had blood tests, MRIs, x-rays, and other tests that "proved" my many conditions. In the past, I looked at that stack of information, and it confirmed what I had always felt, "There is something wrong with me." That all changed when I found out about the power of the mind. After that, I looked at that same stack and was AMAZED! I was SO powerful that I had brilliantly created each one of these conditions and diseases. I was AMAZING! There wasn't anything *wrong* with me, I had just spent my time and energy, creating things that no longer served me. With that knowledge, I began to de-construct all that I had built while also building the future that I wanted.

"Okay, but my disease/illness/ailment is GENETIC!"

Ah-ha! This used to be a deal-breaker. "Well, if it's *genetic*, I guess you're doomed." Not anymore. Through the ground-breaking study of Epigenetics, we now know that genes can be changed! By our thoughts, no less. The belief that we can "pass down" traits from one generation to the next is not a recent theory. We all know that eye color, hair color, and biological dispositions can be passed down genetically....but what if other things can be passed on as well? What if *acquired* traits could follow along to the next generation? Fears, hurts, traumas, addictions. In the late 1700s - early 1800s, Jean-Baptiste Lamarck, a French biologist known for his own theories on evolution, proposed that organisms pass down acquired traits to future generations [1]. Darwin eventually discredited Lamarck's ideas with his belief that "genes do not retain an organism's experiences in a permanently heritable manner." [2]

Science now shows that Lamarck may not have been so far off base. Some of the most fascinating research on this matter comes from the study of children of Holocaust survivors. In 2012, the Department of Psychiatry, São Paulo School of Medicine, published a research article titled, *Transgenerational transmission of trauma and resilience: a qualitative study with Brazilian offspring of Holocaust survivors.* This study concluded by showing that "traumatic experiences can be transmitted to and developed by the second generation." [3]

This study was built off a similar study published in 1997. *Trauma in children of Holocaust survivors: Transgenerational effects,* by Sorscher and Cohen, found that "Holocaust trauma has psychological impacts on the children of survivors, such as higher levels of childhood trauma, increased vulnerability to PTSD, and other psychiatric disorders." [4]

Rachel Yehuda, a professor of psychiatry and neuroscience and the Director of the Traumatic Stress Studies Division at the Mount Sinai School of Medicine, is pioneering some of the latest data with Holocaust survivors. Yehuda states, "Holocaust offspring had the same neuroendocrine or hormonal abnormalities that we were viewing in Holocaust survivors and persons with post-traumatic stress disorder" [5]. Epigenetics sees that genes can be turned on and off and expressed differently, through changes in environment and behavior. Long before I ever considered the mind/body connection, I had my own seemingly epigenetic experience.

In 2001, I was working for an ambulatory equine vet clinic and living on a ranch in Malibu. Every morning before my shift, I would spend time in the clinic restroom throwing up. I had been losing weight and also had menstrual bleeding for about 9 months straight. For any "normal" person, this may have been cause for alarm, but by this point in my life, I was used to random symptoms and frequent ailments. Besides, I didn't have insurance and wasn't making much money. One particular morning, I was riding with the primary doctor of the clinic. Either someone had mentioned my morning ritual or, as a doctor, he began to notice some things were not right with me.

As was part of my illness "program," I was commonly ashamed of ailments. I would mostly "suffer in silence," preferring that I was perceived as strong and healthy. After a little prodding, I came out with my myriad of symptoms, including my bleeding. I had ridden with this doctor many times and knew him to be wise and caring. He immediately suggested that I see a friend of his who was a general practitioner, but he suspected I might have endometriosis. After many tests and 2 surgeries to deal with the endometriosis, I was still unwell. Though the constant bleeding had stopped, I was still throwing up, and now I was also falling asleep at all times of the day...even while driving.

I had gone to visit my cousin who lived in Redondo Beach at the time and she was telling me that she had recently been diagnosed with Celiac disease. After hearing my symptoms, she said I should be tested for Celiac disease because it was genetic. I immediately started eating gluten-free and eventually was able to secure an appointment at a clinic. Very quickly after stopping the gluten, I saw an improvement in my symptoms. It just so happened that my morning breakfast for the last year had been a few slices of sourdough bread with butter. When I finally saw the doctor and explained the different symptoms, my improvement after stopping the gluten, and my cousin's diagnosis, he felt pretty sure that Celiac Disease was also my problem. But he couldn't be sure without an intestinal biopsy.

Again, having no insurance made this impossible. Not to mention that I already had begun improving without any invasive procedures. I thought I had found the answer! What a miracle! Just by avoiding gluten, I could begin to live a "normal" life. I was still referred to a gastroenterologist for follow-up. During my appointment with him, I mentioned that I had no intention of doing the biopsy because it would require that I begin eating gluten again. At this time, the gold standard diagnostic tool was the biopsy, though many advancements have been made in this area. Because

I was opting out of the biopsy, I was given a comprehensive health history instead.

I remember distinctly one of the first questions I was asked, "Did you have any traumatic events happen to you in childhood?" I actually laughed out loud at this question, thinking, "Take your pick, doc!" I briefly explained that "Yes," I had quite a number of traumatic events in childhood, and he nodded and made notes on his paper. This was the first time I had ever been asked anything about my past by a medical professional, besides a medical history. I was caught a little off guard by this and couldn't help but demand an explanation of this intrusive line of questioning. The doctor explained that Celiac Disease was genetic and that certain people are genetically predisposed to developing it. But that it doesn't manifest in everyone that carries the genetic disposition. Research had shown that this gene gets "turned on like a switch" at some point in the person's life [6]. They had linked the "switch being flipped" to traumatic events in people's lives.

At the time, I remember thinking, "Great! Just another little gift from my crummy past! Thanks, Mom and Dad!" Some 15 years later, during the infancy of my journey down the rabbit hole of the mind/body connection, I would remember this doctor's words. It turned out that avoiding gluten wasn't going to be my "miracle cure" because the gluten wasn't exactly the culprit. Even though it was showing up in my "genes." The genetic revolution promised to hold all the answers to health and wellness. Upon discovering the "obesity gene," the "cancer gene," "diabetes gene," and many other possible disease indicators, the scientific and medical communities thought they had found the "holy grail" of information. Unfortunately, it only brought more questions. Why did some people carry the gene for breast cancer and *not* manifest breast cancer, while other women who *didn't* carry the gene *did* develop the disease?

Again, I am taking years of research and science and "dumbing it down" into my personal takeaways. The research on this subject is fascinating and very scientifically dense. It is also still quite controversial. But when I first learned about Epigenetics, my own diagnosis with Celiac Disease came into focus. If traumatic events can "turn on" or influence the disposition of our genes, could they also not be "turned off"? That is my theory and the belief that I operate from. Just as we can remodel a house to suit our preferences and needs, we can also remodel our genes!

My husband and I bought a house in Maui. Though we have had many "fixer-upper" homes in the past, we purchased this home, believing that it only needed minor updates. We were wrong. As we began removing the old Formica countertops to replace them with granite, we quickly realized that everything was not as it seemed. We lifted the old counters just to watch the cabinets below practically disintegrate before our eyes. Years of water and pest damage had left them riddled with rot. Oh, how I wish that were all! We ended up gutting the entire house down to the studs. This was not in the plan. Many hours and dollars later, we had rebuilt everything to our personal taste and quality. It was very comforting *knowing* what was behind each wall because WE put it there. We were building on someone else's foundation. Some of the things were good. The actual framework and foundation were solid. The electrical work was in shambles and not up to code, requiring a complete overhaul.

I thought a lot about our pasts and our minds during the long hours of remodeling, and how similar our lives are to the remodeling of a house. We could have simply left it. We could have patched up the ever-increasing "flaws" that would inevitably pop up. So often, we live our lives like this. "Cracks" show up in our health, and rather than remodel, we patch. We medicate, operate, and succumb to limitations. WE CAN CHANGE...EVEN OUR GENES!!!! By our thoughts and the remodeling of our memories.

"I don't want to dig up the past. Shouldn't I just think positive thoughts?"

People who believe this are under the impression that the "past is in the past." Unfortunately, that is not true. Our present and our future are actually built with the building blocks of our past. I am all for positive thinking. I just spent the last few pages and many other chapters saying that our thoughts can create our realities. But positive thinking, though a clearly-preferable coping mechanism, is still *usually* a coping mechanism. "Yeah, a lot of really horrible things happened to me as a child, but I'm just going to think positive."

What happens in your mind when you do that is this: The conscious mind becomes aware of negative feelings, sensations, pictures, and decides that this is uncomfortable. So it sends the message to think of something different, something positive. The subconscious mind then begins to "weigh" this out. Remember that the subconscious mind is the purely logical and practical part of our mind. If it gets the message that the information is simply "too painful" to deal with, it files it deeply. But it is still there. And each time that a seemingly similar event occurs, the subconscious mind consults these deeper files. Your reactions will be a result of what is filed. So you can continue to bury trauma behind lots of positive thinking, but the scale still tips on the side of pain/fear/sadness. As I mentioned before, it WILL "leak out."

Positive thinking is like putting on a fresh coat of paint. If you paint over a solidly built wall, it looks beautiful and can really enhance the room. If you paint over a wall with cracks or leaks behind it, the paint will soon begin to show the water stains, the mold, the cracks, and the rot. You will have to put on more and more paint. For some people, that is preferable. And that is okay. They have very good reasons for not opening those walls. It can be scary, and it can be a lot of work. Some people don't feel equipped for remodeling. My goal is to give hope to these people, along with the "do-it-yourselfers." The methods I will share with you in Part 2 are simple. You go as fast and as far as you want to. This is YOUR remodel project. Positive thinking plays a huge role in the process. But only after the foundations have been examined and rebuilt if necessary.

"I'm too sick/tired/busy/stressed to do this work."

I would say that you are too sick/tired/busy/stressed NOT to do this work. This can be done from your home, from your bed, on the way to work, or really anywhere you choose. You may need some initial assistance to recognize your power to change...but it's possible. For anyone.

"I don't feel comfortable sharing all the horrible things that were done to me/that I have done."

That's okay. I have helped hundreds of people heal and change their minds without ever knowing what we were working on. Precisely because we are working with your brain. It already knows. Part of the reason I love what I do is because I don't have to know all the "grimy details." I commonly work with people who say to me, "This is something I've never even wanted to admit to *myself*, let alone others."

Listen, I am not a magician. Neither am I a wonderfully intuitive healer. I don't "shift energy," balance chakras, or have any special "miraculous healing gift from God." Many people have ascribed those descriptions to me and the work I do, but I see it a little more simply. I *facilitate*. I help others help themselves. I work with the brain and the mind, and the body follows. It's a much more lucrative business model if I can convince you that you *need me* to make your life better. But it's not the truth. Granted, we all need some help at times, and often we need someone to support us as we transition from the Victim model into the Victor model. But ultimately, the power is in YOUR hands. The power to get well *and* the power to stay exactly where you are.

Why do I say this now? Because no matter what has happened to you, you are not stuck. The work I do is not magic. It's simple and easy to understand once you "get it." I don't need to know the details because *you* already do. Please...don't ever believe you are "too far gone," "too broken," "too indoctrinated." If you have a brain (which I'm going to assume that you do if you are reading this), you can change. Even if you believe that you are past the point of no return, we can change it. Because these methods work with beliefs!

"My childhood was pretty good. I don't really think I have any traumas. How can this help me?"

I am thrilled that you had a good childhood. I have heard this many times, yet the person is in my office. Why? In some ways, it doesn't matter. We all deserve to have the life of our dreams. Are you living it? Great! Drop this book and go enjoy it!! Give it to someone who isn't living their BEST life. These methods can help sick people get well. Diseased people become healthy. Overweight people find the body they can love and accept. It can heal relationships, even with people who have long passed on. It can reverse addictions and mend broken hearts. It can help people become more successful in business, sports, and hobbies.

If you had a great childhood, you are already on your way to having the life you want. But if you need some more tools in your tool-belt, or find that pesky little "programs" keep popping up in your life, this can work for you. That being said, I have worked with numerous clients who made this claim, only to find out it was a lovely little coping mechanism to keep them safe from seeing what really went on in their lives. Again, it's a more socially acceptable and preferable coping skill. Rather than drugs, alcohol, pornography, this person uses the "I had a great childhood, so I have no excuse for feeling the way I do" skill. But if this isn't "true" in any part of their internal resources, it will find a way to "leak out" eventually.

These are the individuals who "have everything" and yet keep up the relentless pursuit for MORE. The high power executive who never "found the time" to get married or have a relationship of any worth. The mental health guru who now develops a debilitating disease. The healthy, fit marathon runner who drops dead of a heart attack at age 45.

It doesn't have to be a traumatic childhood. It can be war, heartbreak, loss of a loved one, a natural disaster. It can be religious trauma, a car accident, or betrayal from a close friend. I'd like to share the story of a client named Amanda to illustrate this point.

AMANDA

Amanda was referred to me because she was a 40-year-old woman with 4 kids, and she didn't drive. It had caused great strain on her marriage, especially as her children reached school age and the driving demands became increasingly difficult for her husband to manage alone. In the initial consultation, I believed that Amanda had never learned to drive and had no desire to learn. She was terrified at the very idea. She had even begun to fear the very idea of riding in a car and would sit nearly paralyzed with fear as her husband drove, screaming with every bump or turn.

When Amanda arrived for the session, dropped off by her husband, I was met with a small, timid woman. She carefully averted her gaze and was clearly nervous about our time together. As always, I took an inventory of past experiences and found that Amanda had a happy and loving childhood. Other than the occasional sibling squabble, she could only remember positive experiences growing up. When I further investigated her driving experiences, I found that she actually had learned to drive and obtained her license at 16. When Amanda was 17, she was driving and had hit a patch of wet road, and the car spun out of control. Nobody was hurt, but it frightened her tremendously. This was not enough to cause the full-blown phobia I was witnessing before me, so I probed deeper. Amanda grew visibly more anxious and practically shrunk into her seat as she began recalling the next memory. At 18, Amanda was a passenger in a car with her brother. As they drove through town, a bicyclist suddenly appeared on Amanda's side of the car. Her brother did not see the cyclist in time and hit the man.

With great detail, Amanda recalled feeling the tires run over the man and his bike. It was clear to me that she was reliving the incident. I stopped her, knowing that we had already found the source of her phobia. Going into further details was not necessary at this time. Amanda was representing this trauma visually in her mind. She had very clear pictures, and as is common with rehearsed traumatic events, she also had clear sounds and feelings associated with this event.

I had a colleague working with me during this particular session and we quickly began addressing the trauma she was experiencing. After a relatively short amount of time, she began to relax, and soon we were able to allow her to view the story and event without being in the situation. We worked on every aspect of the accident, the pictures, the sounds, and the feelings. Soon, she was able to begin re-telling the story in a different way. Seeing things the way she would have liked to have seen them and making peace with her brother, the man, and herself.

Will This Work for Me?

Knowing that a well-rehearsed traumatic memory can be stored physically within the body, I knew we needed to clear that as well. So I signaled to my colleague that I was about to tip Amanda's chair a little as she was in the trance of her story. We had cleared enough of the trauma at this point that I felt sure that she would be able to handle this without regressing back to the original state. This was important to do because without addressing this, she could easily be triggered back into a part of this event with even the smallest bump in the road. Our goal is always to be as thorough as possible with these memories, not leaving any "negative information" within the files.

As Amanda began walking us through the new memory, I took her chair and gave it a quick jostle. Amanda immediately screamed and grabbed the arms of the chair for dear life. Expecting this reaction, we immediately addressed the physical memory and calmed down her system, re-training her mind and body with a new reaction. I kept tipping the chair, jostling it harder and harder each time. Within minutes, Amanda was squealing with joy as she naturally linked this movement to the excitement of riding a roller coaster rather than running over a man.

Within two hours, Amanda was transformed. Toward the end of the session, she began sitting up in her chair, rather than the reclusive slouching position she had held in the beginning. She also removed her low ponytail, and her hair flowed naturally to her shoulders. Suddenly, this soft-spoken and shy woman blossomed into a chatty and vibrant individual. We moved the session outside into one of the vehicles. First, having her sit in the passenger side without the car being started. We ensured that no negative associations arose, but instead, feelings of

156

excitement and power. When we were sure that she was successful, we moved her into the driver's seat, again without the car being started. We had her go through the motions of starting the car, buckling her belt, and pretending to drive around the neighborhood. At one point, she had her arm out the window as she imagined the breeze blowing through her air as she drove down the freeway. She was laughing and enjoying herself. We asked her if she was ready to drive, and she enthusiastically agreed. Of course, without having a license, we didn't feel that it would be an actual option.

About this time, her husband arrived to pick Amanda up from the session. He was in complete shock at what he was seeing! We decided to test out her new neuropathways even further. We enlisted her husband to help. I quietly pulled him to the side and asked him to drive us around the neighborhood, but with a few minor adjustments. I asked him to brake suddenly at times and swerve dramatically once in a while. Amanda jumped into the passenger side, and my colleague and I got into the back, letting her know we would be there to help her through any residual anxiety.

Upon the first sudden slam on the breaks, Amanda instinctively braced herself and reached for the safety bar while letting out a little yelp. We quickly worked with her through this and moved along. Within minutes, Amanda was easily navigating the quick stops and the sudden swerves with laughter. Even letting out a boisterous "WEEEEEE!" at one particular swerve, immediately connecting to the roller coaster feeling.

After our adventurous ride, we made a plan for Amanda to enroll in a driving course and work toward getting her license. Her husband was speechless and could barely believe what he was seeing. We gave Amanda some "homework," which was just exercises in strengthening her fledgling neuropathways and replaying the new memory. I followed up with Amanda later, and she happily reported that she was enrolled in a driving course and would likely be getting her license soon.

Amanda didn't have a traumatic childhood, but she did have a traumatic event. Though she knew that particular experience was not one that she liked to think about, she had no idea how much power it had over her. See, every time she was faced with the idea of driving or riding in a car, she likely played that memory in her subconscious mind. She had to have a very good reason for not driving, and her mind offered up a landslide of pictures/emotions/feelings to support that choice. Now, though she knows that event happened in the past, she no longer has the pictures/feelings/sensations/sounds/smells to support it. She has something different there instead. Now, she automatically produces a different response to the idea of driving.

"I don't really want to change my memories. They make me who I am. Who will I be without my memories?" / "Won't I be lying to myself if I change a memory?"

First of all, it's important to remember that memory isn't "real" anyway. It has been irrevocably changed by your own perceptions, filters, and experiences. WE don't "take away" memory, and we also don't make fairytales up in your mind. We clear negative associations so that you can see clearly what you need to keep and what you can release. Remember, what you hold within is what you give to others. So, then the question is, do you like what is currently being produced in your life? If so, great! If not, then it makes sense to go back and let go of what doesn't serve you and give yourself something better. Don't you deserve that? It's YOUR mind, you get to choose what you keep and what you let go of.

"I don't really have the money to spend on getting sessions or getting trained on how to do these techniques."

It is important to realize that a "lack" in finances is almost always a program related to money. The way we feel about money and the relationship we have with finances is closely related to the way we feel about ourselves. It's very similar to our relationship with food. Interestingly enough, I had the same thought when it came to this information. I had been on disability for years, my husband and I had spent nearly $100,000 out of pocket on my health challenges over the years. We were not in a financial place to spend any more money.

But I was scheduled to have yet another spinal surgery, and I was going for IV infusions every other day. I was on close to 180 meds, supplements, and tinctures EVERY DAY until my liver and kidneys gave out. **It was costing me an astronomical amount of money to stay sick.** Even with very good insurance, I actually couldn't afford to continue to support myself in the illness.

My question would be, *can you afford NOT to get help?* I had to face this exact same dilemma. I can now safely say that I would have paid triple the amount of money I had to learn this material. More, in fact. This information is priceless. I totally understand that financial duress is a very real thing. Anyone can learn and utilize these tools. That is my ultimate goal with this book—to make this knowledge and these tools accessible for anyone. Again, some problems are more complex and may need an expert to get the ball rolling. But these tools were never meant to line a practitioner's pocket. My goal is ALWAYS to equip my clients with the ability to do this work themselves.

"I've tried EFT/Hypnosis/Therapy/EMDR/FEFT/etc. and it didn't work for me. How is this any different?"

Obviously, without knowing you personally, I cannot speak to your experiences. What I can say is that I get many clients that come from other modalities; even practitioners of these modalities often come to me for help. Is it that these modalities are ineffective? I would say no. Most of the information contained in this book comes from the application and research associated with these techniques. I have found extremely valuable tools from each one of the methods.

What I believe makes Mind Change even quicker and effective is that I have endeavored to find out *WHY* the things that *do* work, work. Each of these systems (and more) have made incredible contributions in the field of health and wellness. So, like many before me, I have "cherry-picked" the best of each system and put them together so that mind/body/science all converge to give you the best possible tools for changing your life.

On a side note, it's important to remember that for some people, they have spent 20, 30 or 40+ years developing the coping skills that they are now using. These things rarely fall apart overnight (although they can). But think about it, let's say it's taken you 20 years to build a phobia, or a disease, or an addiction that has been practiced, unconsciously, daily for 20 years. You are an expert at it. But now, you are ready for something different. We are now on the journey to *dis-assemble* the very coping mechanism that has "kept you safe" all these years. That is no small feat! But it is more than doable.

If you can address the root cause, the secondary gains associated AND have a properly-constructed *alternative* outcome…it is rare to have Mind Change *not work*. Also, please refer back to the first question in this section. It's possible that you may be running the "nothing works for me" program. If that is the case, *that* belief would need to be dealt with first. Otherwise, you will keep producing the result of things "not working." We are incredibly powerful creators!!

Also, don't forget the RAS (Reticular Activating System) discussed in Chapter 4. When you ask the question, "What if this *doesn't* work for me?" your mind WILL answer that question. You will start to fantasize all of the adverse outcomes, and you will further reinforce all the "danger" associated with trying to change. Even if you take the leap and try, the RAS will begin looking for what you are focused on…all the ways this is *not* working. The RAS is like a bloodhound! It ALWAYS finds what it's looking for. Does this sound familiar? Have you tried to change before and found this to be the case?

Luckily, Mind Change deals with beliefs. Therefore we can start to ask better questions for your mind to answer. What if this *does* work? If the mind finds any "good" reasons that it wouldn't be safe for it to work, we can deal with that as well! Really, it's a win/win situation. The only people I have experienced that these techniques have not worked for are those who find more *benefit in staying where they are* rather than changing. The problem is, they are not consciously aware of that "benefit." The investment they have in their particular "problem" is too great at this point. Please hear me say this...there is NO judgment on these people.

We simply cannot trump our subconscious programming by desire alone. Thank goodness, as our subconscious programming is responsible for 90% of our daily vital functions. I don't know about you, but my desires change by the hour! Sometimes, even more frequently. If my conscious mind ruled...I would be a hot mess! The good thing is, we can work together. Having congruency with the subconscious and conscious mind means a balanced life. For those who are ready, the tools are there.

"If all of this information is true, why haven't I heard about it before?"

Again, I'm going to have to reference the RAS. Just wait, after reading this book, or even in the process of reading it, you will begin to notice how many people ARE talking about it. You'll overhear conversations, see interviews, listen to a podcast. Believe me, you will start to hear more about it as you begin to listen.

That being said, we are in a constant state of evolution. New developments in science and technology are happening daily. We understand so much more about the brain than we did 20 years ago. We typically wait for science and PhDs to study, research, experiment, and then "dumb-it-down" enough for the general public to digest it. Innovation and information happen almost *too* fast these days. It's difficult to keep up! Our entire social structure is set up in a way that we wait for *authorities* to tell us what to do, what to eat, what to believe. Then when they figure out what they have been saying is wrong; they just tell us that "research *now shows*" something else, and we blindly follow.

Just look at smoking and the tobacco industry. Or the food pyramid. What was originally told to us is far different than the current recommendations. Obviously, it wouldn't be "news" to you to say that the almighty dollar plays a massive role in what we hear as a general public. I have no intention to get all "conspiracy theory" with what I'm about to say, so don't read too much into it. But, the things that I am saying and the tools that I have to offer are not going to EVER be very popular. Why? For the most part, nobody can monetize it. My sole intention is to give the power back to *you*. If the power to be happy, well, successful, is in YOUR hands, there is no single person or entity that can "corner the market" on that.

If no drug, no therapist, no facility, no food group or supplement holds the power to your wellness, then nobody makes a fortune off of you getting better. If there is no money, there is no research. If there is no research, there is no "proof" that these methods work. Which means, it's likely that you will not be hearing about this from the "medical world" anytime soon. So, the burden of response relies solely upon where it needs to be....in your lap. For those who are willing to accept that their *personal* healing is just that, personal, they are already one step ahead of the game. For those who are still giving their power away to some "higher authority," they will continue to wait for the right pill, diet, surgery, or guru.

Will This Work for Me?

The previous questions are just a few of the many "concerns" that I have encountered. Obviously, I cannot address all of them here. But for a moment, I would ask you to suspend any further judgment until you have fully processed all of the information held in these pages. The changing of one's mind is no small feat, be patient with yourself. It is time to transition from the "why" to the "how." In Part 2, I will discuss "how" to take control back and change your mind.

PART 2

Mind Change Method

CHAPTER 11

Mind Change Method

"You're not stuck. You're just committed to certain patterns of behavior because they helped you in the past. Now those behaviors have become more harmful than helpful. The reason why you can't move forward is because you keep applying an old formula to a new level in your life. Change the formula to get a different result."

Emily Maroutian

I'm beginning to suspect that the second half of life is about learning to let go of everything I feverishly collected over the first half that wasn't loving or human."

Michael Xavier

What Is Mind Change?

If you are anything like me, you are ready for the "meat and potatoes"! In fact, you may have even skipped ahead to this part of the book to see if the practicals of this method are appealing to you or "something you have already tried." Again, I get it! If that is you, I will appeal to you to please go back and read the rest before you move on. Though *knowing* the "How & Why" we do what we do is rarely powerful enough to change it; I have found that it really sets the mind up for change.

I have broken Part 2 into easy to understand, actionable practicals. I would suggest reading through everything first, at least once before applying them. Again, I believe in the power of seeing the "macro" version of the entire process before diving in. If I may use the old adage, "failing to plan is planning to fail!" One of the most prominent overarching themes to "self-work" is almost always: Love. Love yourself enough to take the time and energy to invest in this process. AND, be loving to yourself in the process.

Remember, the things you want to change are a result of subconsciously "practicing" them for years, sometimes decades or even lifetimes! Considering the ideas behind Epigenetics, these things may have been passed down over centuries. Having a Mind Change about your problem, life, or disease takes considerably less time to change than it did to build, but still, give yourself the time and space to do so. Let's address THE most common question I get with the work I do:

"How long will it take for me to change my problem?"

Mind Change

I don't know. Because your "problem" is unique to you and your programming, I can't say. Two people can come to see me with nearly identical issues, and the time it takes for resolution of the problem will differ significantly because no two "problems" are built the same. What I can say is that, in my experience, these methods provide the fastest route to change I have ever encountered. Problems *can* change within one session. I see that happen all the time. It was my personal experience. Within one session, my life was forever altered. People from all over the world who have heard my story always ask me the same question, "How were you able to heal so quickly? What did you do?" I always say that it came down to one clear understanding: *I was doing it to me.* And rather than get defensive (like I normally would have) and start trying to defend how "real" my issues were and all the medical "proof" I had that I was dying, I made a life-changing decision to CHANGE MY MIND. Blaming it on other people or *things* wasn't working for me. I had beat that horse to the ground. So "what if" it *was* me? For the first time, maybe in my life, I felt empowered. If I was doing it, I could stop it. So I believed. I changed my mind completely, and it gave me the power. This time, the power to create the life of my dreams instead of countless rare diseases. The power to finally "deal" with my past and stop running from it.

In the following chapters, we will lay out a step-by-step plan to help you change your mind!

- **Mind Change Manifesto:** this will help you identify exactly what you would like to see in your future so that you can know where you are going.

- **Mind Change GPS:** this will be your "directions" and tools to get where you are going. We will teach you how to utilize your **G**ratitude, **P**ositive Affirmations, and Happy Memories (**S**miles) to begin creating your dreams.
- **PaNE CuRe List:** this is a powerful tool that will help you identify the past negative experiences, limiting beliefs, as well as programs that are keeping you stuck in some of your unpleasant patterns.
- **Pattern Interrupts:** learning this tool and the power behind it is a key piece to overcoming the things holding you back.
- **The Process:** utilizing all of the above tools, we break down the Mind Change Method into a simple to use program to help you take the power back in your own life!

Mind Change is not for the timid. It is for the brave. The few people ready to "take on" everything they *think* they know and turn it upside down will tap into a power that they only dreamed possible. The hardest and best knowledge we must face is that we have a choice.

I love the Matrix movies. If you haven't seen them, please put down this book and go and watch the first one. They were profoundly ahead of their time and still remain underrated. Mind Change is like the Matrix. You won't be able to "unknow" this information, this power. You can continue to run from it, but it will be like the little unscratchable itch in your brain. What if? What if *you* have the power? I leave you with these little nuggets from the Matrix. See you on the other side!

Mind Change

"This is your last chance. After this, there is no turning back. You take the blue pill - the story ends, you wake up in your bed and believe whatever you want to believe. You take the red pill - you stay in Wonderland, and I show you how deep the rabbit-hole goes...I'm trying to free your mind, Neo. But I can only show you the door. You're the one that has to walk through it"

Morpheus: The Matrix

CHAPTER 12

The Perfectly Working You

"The reason why the world lacks unity, and lies broken and in heaps, is, because man is disunited with himself."

Ralph Waldo Emerson

"The body is the servant of the mind. It obeys the operations of the mind, whether they be deliberately chosen or automatically expressed."

James Allen, As a Man Thinketh

Mind Change

The first thing I would like to remind you of is this...there is likely nothing *wrong* with you. No, I'm not saying that your problem is "only in your head." I believe and know from experience, that the body can produce very "real" symptoms, diseases, feelings, and emotions in accordance to what is going on with us. You may have stage 4 cancer, or an MS diagnosis, or lupus and have turned to this information as a "last-ditch effort." I am here to say I know the fear, pain, and uncertainty that accompanies physical dis-ease. But that doesn't necessarily mean something is *malfunctioning* within you. On the contrary, you are likely working perfectly according to the way we function as humans. If you persist with the belief that "something is wrong with me," then your body (who is the obedient slave to the mind) WILL eventually produce something that will prove you right and may have already taken that route.

Hopefully, if you read Part 1, you now know that what we contain in our subconscious "filing system" is supporting and feeding our automatic Mode of Operation. So, if you are ill, depressed, anxious, or producing dis-ease...you have a very good reason for doing it. This is *the* very important FIRST STEP in changing your mind.

Remember I mentioned before that we remodeled the house I am living in now. There are a couple of things that are little "quirks" in my home. For instance, though we had a lot of electrical rewiring done (the original wiring was a complete mess), there were a few things we left alone. One of those things is the light switch for the dining room. This particular light is actually wired into two different panels, each with a master-switch. This means it can be shut off and turned on from two panels in two different locations. So I often spend a few minutes trying to figure out which switch is flipped which way so that I can get the silly light to turn on. So here is the question...is my light switch "broken"? No, it's not. It's performing exactly the way it was wired. Unfortunately, it wasn't wired for optimal performance. But it is NOT broken. If this bothered me enough, I would simply "rewire" it to produce the desired outcome. Frankly, I have far more important concerns in my life!

I also have a faucet on my bathroom sink that we replaced. When we installed it, we accidentally put the HOT water handle on the cold water line. Again, NOT broken. Just installed incorrectly. Are you with me? Many of us have original hardware that just needs some remodeling. It isn't working optimally. That's okay. We just need to rewire. Sometimes it's not even that significant. We simply want to upgrade! Guess what? Go for it! It's YOUR mind and YOUR body. Make it as great as you choose.

Even though the Mind Change Method is based on years of experience, research, and science, it's a simple tool. Taking power back over the way your body and/or emotions respond is relatively easy. Overcoming the fears, doubts, and victim-conditioning is not. No matter what your background, health limitations, diagnosis, or situation, you can learn to think differently. Stop believing the lie that you are "broken." Might you need some rewiring? Probably. Welcome to the club. I want you to take some time and answer the following questions:

1. What have I learned so far that will empower me to Change my Mind?

2. How has my mind changed already?

3. What tools have I gained from this book and from my life that will make me successful in changing my mind?

4. How do I know that I am ready to use the Mind Change Method to take my power back and live my best life?

I'm trusting that you took the time to complete that exercise. How was it? Whether you are aware of it or not, these answers provide the building blocks that are already at work in your subconscious mind that will facilitate the change. I want you to become aware of some of the patterns and beliefs that emerge as you go through this process.

I would like to give you a simple equation, that if understood and applied, holds the power of changing nearly anything. Ready?

RUMINATION + DECLARATION = CREATION

Rumination

Let's break this down a little. First off, RUMINATION. Rumination is defined by Webster's Dictionary as:

1. A deep or considered thought about something.

2. The action or process of thinking deeply about something.

Rumination is one of the hallmarks of the mind. It is simply our thoughts that occur over and over again. Sometimes those thoughts are in our conscious awareness, sometimes subconscious. Regardless, they are the building blocks for our belief systems. Also known as the "little voice inside my head," the "broken record," or the "phrase/picture/sound that keeps popping into my head," these are ruminations. Often times, we think these thoughts so often that they seem naturally "hard-wired" into our thinking. Ruminations are not "good" or "bad." They are just thoughts. If we judge our thoughts, we are simply thinking more thoughts about our thoughts. Make sense? Let me illustrate.

You are rushing out the door in the morning and realize you cannot find your keys. As you frantically search, thoughts fill your mind. "I can't believe I did this again! I'm such an idiot," "Great! Now I'm going to be even more late and probably get fired," "This kind of thing ALWAYS happens to me," and so on. If you were to take a time-out and reflect on these thoughts, you probably would agree that they are not the most productive thoughts if you are trying to find your keys, feel good, and get going. You may even go as far as beating yourself up over these thoughts. Now, you are thinking, "I'm such a bully to myself," "I know better than to let negative thinking get in my way, what an idiot I am," "I will never be able to stop being so hard on myself."

See? Those are just thoughts *about* your thoughts. Generally, not helpful. What if, on the other hand, you were to take a time-out and listen. Rather than judge the thoughts, take a moment to hear what they are saying. Notice them. They are there for a reason. They are your creation from past experiences. Your beliefs. It's so helpful to know what we ruminate about. This is invaluable feedback! Becoming aware of what we ruminate on can enable us to make better choices. We are the gatekeepers of our minds. We only need to let in what we want. Remember the garden analogy? Your mind is your garden. It's wonderful that weeds pop up and show themselves. Why? Because then I can pull them out! Luckily, the weeds aren't happening underground where I can't see them.

Otherwise, I may not know they are there. If something is in my garden that either I didn't plant, or I no longer want to grow there, it makes no sense for me to "judge" it. I can just as easily pull it out with a happy and grateful mood, knowing that my garden will be better for it.

Ruminations are like seeds in our garden. With food and water, some will grow up to be nourishing, beautiful plants. Others will grow up to reveal the weed that they are. Once we are aware of what they are, we can keep them or pluck them out! Ruminations are powerful and can ultimately dictate many of our feelings and behaviors, but combined with the next step...they are incredibly powerful.

Declaration

Declaration is formally and confidently announcing something. Usually, this is a verbal act, though it can also be a nonverbal declaration. A large smile can be a declaration of happiness or humor. A raised fist can be a declaration that says, "You better run, or I'll clobber you!" Declarations are usually a result of our ruminations, but now, we are formally announcing them. Plucked from our minds, we now speak them into existence. Giving them a voice and allowing them to be heard.

Remember back to "what is real." If we can touch it, taste it, hear it, and/or see it, it is "real." By speaking this thought into existence *outside* of our body, you are now giving it life and an opportunity to become "real." Are you beginning to see just how powerful you are? Your mouth spoke it, but your ears heard it. The body likely responded to a feeling that was created to deal with what it just heard. None of us like to be liars, even if you are someone who commonly uses it as a coping skill. If we say it, it must be true. At least to some part of us. When you speak the words, "I am an idiot!," or "Nobody loves me," or "Life is so unfair. This always happens to me," you are moving to the next step of creating its truth.

When we "declare" something, we are activating numerous powerful systems within our mind and body. The system regulating hormones needs to produce "feeling" in alignment with what is being declared. The RAS (reticular activating system) is brought online to began looking for other "proof" that this is true. The subconscious filing system is now searching through all of its data to figure out where this should be filed and looks for similar occurrences, which only reinforces the negative cycle.

Creation

If we are ruminating on things that do not serve us, then declaring them, we are creating. We may feel "set in our ways," but we are constantly creating. Often, we are busy creating more of what we already have, simply practicing old beliefs/patterns/feelings. In essence, what we are creating is the illusion of being "stuck." But we *are* creating, nonetheless.

We are the Master Designers of our life. But we often outsource this important job to others around us. Letting them dictate our worth and value. Collecting other people's hurts, pains, and experiences and making them our own. Or choosing to hold on to our own hurts and pains and allowing them to define us. Consider the story of a friend of mine who was diagnosed with kidney stones. She had passed a few with relatively little discomfort and was advised that the rest should pass similarly. Returning to work the next day, she told many of her coworkers about the diagnosis. Instantly, she was inundated with horror stories of other people's experiences with kidney stones. "It's worse than giving birth!" one coworker related. "I peed blood for days and felt like I was going to die!" another said dramatically. Yet another coworker shared the story of her brother who ended up having complications with kidney stones and ended up having a seizure!

That whole day, my friend ruminated on these things. Her coworkers repeatedly checked on her, asking her how she was feeling. Each time, she realized and expressed that she was feeling worse. By the time she was ready to end her workday, she was feeling lousy. She called her husband, "I think I'm having complications. I'm feeling a lot of strange symptoms." Not surprisingly, she ended up in the emergency room that night in a great deal of pain. The next day, she followed up with her regular doctor, who seemed surprised at her turn for the worse. In fact, x-rays had revealed that the rest of the stones had resolved and had probably passed the day before. How did she do this? Simple:

RUMINATION + DECLARATION = CREATION

But guess what? The opposite is true as well! What do you think if you ruminated on how *good* you feel? How much you have to be grateful for and all the ways that this is true. If you woke up in the morning knowing it was going to be a good day and declaring it to be so, could you also *create* that good day? I utilized this process in my healing journey. After realizing that I had the power to create health in my body, just as I had created disease, I began to ruminate on it. I thought "healthy" thoughts. "How am I going to move my body today?" "How am I going to feed this body that is healthy?" "What kinds of things do I want to do with my healthy body?" I also declared my healing. Numerous people were aware of how bad my health had deteriorated and would frequently check up on me or inquire as to my wellbeing when we would see each other. "I'm healed!" I would exclaim brightly. "I'm just waiting for my body to catch up!" "Of course I *can* do _____!" "I love to walk/run/workout. It makes me feel so good." And rather quickly, this became natural and normal. Within 4 months of being practically bedridden and near death, I was in the gym leg pressing almost 450 lbs.

This goes beyond positive thinking. This is being very intentional but also very observational. If we can understand that the majority of the situations we find ourselves in are *our creation*, then we conversely understand that we also have the power to create something different.

You see, the first step to changing your mind is to understand that you are working perfectly in accordance with the equation:

RUMINATION + DECLARATION = CREATION

If we know that we can create our environment by observing and changing our ruminations and declarations, why don't we? Often, we don't know how. And if we do, we have strong and powerful "objections" to our desired outcomes. This is where the next step comes in.

CHAPTER 13

Mind Change Manifesto

*"If you don't know where you are going,
you'll end up someplace else."*

Yogi Berra, former New York Yankees catcher

*"Our goals can only be reached through a vehicle of a plan, in
which we must fervently believe, and upon which we must
vigorously act. There is no other route to success."*

Pablo Picasso

Arguably, the most crucial step of Mind Change is changing your mind! For many people, it is difficult to see beyond what is directly in front of them. Many people *want* a better life. They want a healthy body, a happy marriage, a good job, financial security. They "hope" and "wish." But, I've learned that it can be difficult for people to see this actually play out in their future.

One of the questions I usually ask my clients before we begin working to change their mind, is this: WHAT DO YOU WANT? It sounds like a relatively easy question, right? Let me give you an example of what I am talking about with an example conversation. Let's say that Ronda comes to see me. Ronda is sick with numerous autoimmune disorders, Multiple Chemical Sensitivities (MCS), and fibromyalgia.

RONDA

Ronda: I am just so sick. I can barely leave my house. Everything seems to trigger my MCS. I am bothered by everything. The smell of laundry detergent triggers extreme fatigue and panic. I can't leave the house because the smog bothers me. People's perfume bothers me. I can even smell people's deodorant from five feet away, and it makes me sick! I can feel the EMFs (electromagnetic fields) everywhere! I'm sure there is mold in my house, and I am reacting to it. My body hurts everywhere. I used to be very active, but now, even getting out of bed is painful. I rarely feel well. I can't take care of my house, because every cleaning scent bothers me. I can't take care of my children because I just don't have the energy. I can't work because every smell causes me to get worse. I can barely even go to the doctor's office anymore because of the fluorescent lighting. Not to mention all the chemical smells there. I don't think I will ever get better. In fact, I am just getting worse every day!

Me: So, Ronda, what do you want?

Ronda: I don't want to feel sick anymore! I don't want every smell to bother me. I don't want to watch my children grow up around me but not be able to really be with them. I don't want to wake up feeling tired and sore. I don't want to get worse every day. I don't want smells and foods and lights to bother me. I don't want to live like this!

*Me: So, Ronda, I hear what you **don't** want. What **do** you want?*

Ronda: (looking slightly confused) I told you. I don't want to be sick anymore. I don't want to be robbed of my life and my children. I don't want to miss out on my life!

*Me: Ronda, that is what you **don't** want. The things you **already have**. What do you want different? What **do** you want?*

Ronda: Okay, well, I guess I want to be well. I don't want to feel this way anymore. I want my old life back. I want things to go back to the way they were before I got sick.

Ronda is not alone. I can't begin to explain how common this interaction is. Do you see the problem? Ronda is very well versed in what she **doesn't want**. In fact, she could fill pages of what she no longer wants to do, feel, experience. But when given a chance to see outside of those things, she quickly circles back to what she knows. Why is that? It's rather simple. We are comfortable with what we know, even if it's extremely "uncomfortable." Many times, we cannot *see* a way out of where we are. We just know we want out. We've all heard the famous quote from Ben Franklin, *"By failing to prepare, you are preparing to fail."* This is true for so many reasons.

Simply put, we can't go where we don't know. If I told you about the Land of Flisse, and somehow convinced you that you needed to go there, how would you go about getting started? Even if you *really, really* want to get there, you need a starting place. First of all, what the heck is the "Land of Flisse"? Well, I just made it up. But it illustrates the point. Many people who are in the depths of their problem will face the same problem as you would with the Land of Flisse. It seems like a fairytale. They are so unfamiliar with it that they cannot begin to conceive what the first step would even be. It's easy to judge this idea or the people. "Come on, how hard is it to envision feeling well? Weren't you well at one time? It's not like that is a made-up place!" True. But for some people, their reality has been this other place for so long that it truly seems impossible to see outside of it. But seeing outside of it is really the first step to getting outside of it.

Power Of Visualization

The power of visualization is far from a "new-age," "woo-woo" concept. As far back as 450 BC, Thucydides, an early Greek philosopher, said these words, "The bravest are surely those who have the clearest vision of what is before them, glory and danger alike, and yet notwithstanding, go out to meet it." The power of our minds to create our future has been utilized for centuries.

Mind Change

A popular documentary on this subject is called "The Secret." In this film, numerous authors, philosophers, and scientists explain the concepts of visualizing your goals. Denis Waitley, Ph.D., a psychologist featured in the film, relates how he was inspired by the use of visualization in the Apollo Mission [1]. Based on his findings, he decided to use the power of visualization in the 1980s and 1990s Olympics programs. After the great success of this exercise, Waitley stated, "When you visualize, then you materialize. And the interesting thing about the mind is…we took Olympic athletes, and then hooked them up to sophisticated biofeedback equipment, and had them run their event only in their mind. Incredibly, the same muscles fired in the same sequence when they were running the race in their minds as when they were running on the track. How could this be? Because the mind cannot distinguish whether you're really doing it, or whether it's just a practice. I believe if you've been there in the mind, you'll go there in the body too." [2]

Let's look at a few well-known examples of people who harnessed the power of visualization:

- Air Force Colonel George Hall: A Vietnam POW, Hall was held in a North Vietnamese prison for seven years, suffering unthinkable conditions. To pass the time, Hall would play a full game of golf in his mind. Going through each motion meticulously. Arriving at the green, selecting his club and making each shot. After being released from the POW camp, he entered the Greater New Orleans Open and shot a 76. This was **one week** after his release!

- Vera Fryling, M.D.: Fryling was a teenager when she was hiding in Berlin during the Holocaust. Being a Jew, Fryling was staying undercover just to stay alive. While hiding, Fryling passed the time by imagining that she was a doctor. She dreamed of becoming a psychiatrist in a free land, practicing the images and feelings over and over again. Not surprisingly, Fryling ended up escaping the Nazis and went on to become a member of the faculty at the San Francisco School of Medicine.

- Nikola Tesla: Said to be the inventor of the modern world, Tesla was a prolific creator. It is said that before he ever sketched a single idea, he would first spend months to years visualizing it. Tesla would change the construction, make improvements, and even operate the device mentally. He could accurately give the measurements of all parts to workmen, simply from the mental construction. When completed, all the parts will fit, just as if they had been drawn to specification. Tesla would even test his innovations in his mind, feeling that this practice was equally as valuable as actual testing. Tesla claimed that the inventions he conceived in this way always worked.

- Jim Carrey: As early as Carrey could remember, he wanted to be an actor. In the early 1990s, Carrey was still an unknown actor and struggling to get by. One day, Carrey decided to write a check to himself for $10 million. He wrote the date for 1994, and on the bottom of the check he wrote, "for acting services rendered." He reportedly carried it in his wallet for daily inspiration. Carrey was later cast for one of the leads in Dumb and Dumber. He found out that he would make a salary of $10 million for that movie. It was shot in 1994.

The stories go on and on. Professional athletes, famous sports teams, singers, and people given fatal diagnoses, all using the power of visualization to achieve their goals. But everyone knows someone who this *didn't* work for. Maybe even you. Many just chalk this up to luck or privilege. But what if we all possess this ability, but have yet to actually harness it? Let's look at some of the key pieces to utilizing this power to begin to create our best life.

It's So Hard To Think Good

Professor Roy Baumeister, a social psychologist at Florida State University, states the following in his published article regarding negative thinking:

"The greater power of bad events over good ones is found in everyday events, major life events (e.g., trauma), close relationship outcomes, social network patterns, interpersonal interactions, and learning processes. Bad emotions, bad parents, and bad feedback have more impact than good ones, and bad information is processed more thoroughly than good. The self is more motivated to avoid bad self-definitions than to pursue good ones. Bad impressions and bad stereotypes are quicker to form and more resistant to disconfirmation than good ones." [3]

Remembering back to Chapter 5 when we discussed how memories are formed, you may recall that more of our senses are engaged when a "bad" memory is being processed. Because of our primal inclination toward safety, anything that is perceived as a threat engages our sensory inputs in a more acutely.   Also, the quality of our current life is almost solely dictated by the way we perceive the events that shaped us.   So, if we view our past in a more negative light, it stands to reason that we are fine-tuned to see the negative in every situation.   That takes us squarely back to our Victim Model of thinking, discussed in Chapter 3.

But just as you *learned* to perceive the negative by practicing it, you can also learn to perceive the positive.   Whichever you do more will ultimately be the winning perception.   You may have heard the old adage of the Two Wolves:

An old Cherokee is teaching his grandson about life:

"A fight is going on inside me," the old man said to the boy.

"It is a terrible fight, and it is between two wolves. One is evil—he is anger, envy, sorrow, regret, greed, arrogance, self-pity, guilt, resentment, inferiority, lies, false pride, superiority, and ego."

He continued, "The other is good—he is joy, peace, love, hope, serenity, humility, kindness, benevolence, empathy, generosity, truth, compassion, and faith."

"The same fight is going on inside you—and inside every other person, too."

The grandson thought about it for a minute and then asked his grandfather: "Which wolf will win?"

The old Cherokee simply replied, "The one you feed."

This beloved fable illustrates our choice in a winning perception. We must choose what we think, what we focus on, and what we create. Visualization is a powerful tool.

How To Visualize Your Future

Are you resistant to this practice? The fact is, you already do it. Probably every day. Are you sick? Every night, you likely go to bed, wondering how you will feel the next morning. You visualize the worst-case scenario. "Will I feel worse?" Will a new symptom appear?" You actually begin to create visual pictures or feelings in your body to represent your tomorrow. You are creating! Good job. But do you like the outcome? No? Change it!

I have worked with countless insomniacs. The biggest problem with insomniacs is the *fear* of not sleeping. Nearly every day, they think about that night. "Will I sleep?" How long will it last tonight?" I've even known people who come up with a list of things to do that night—while they are *not sleeping*! Talk about planning. Everything becomes a trigger to *not* sleep. Even the bedroom becomes a place that is uncomfortable because of the thoughts of "no sleep" it evokes. They have a detailed plan on "how *not* to sleep" that night. And the body follows!

The single most common defense I hear for this type of planning is, "But I don't want to be disappointed when _____ doesn't happen!" Do you see? Even the defense is in alignment with what you expect to happen. People feel the need to be "prepared" for the worst.

Unfortunately, this usually ends up creating the very thing they say they don't want.

Now, hear me say this. For many people, just the act of visualization is enough to create an alternate outcome. For others, they have very good reasons for holding onto all the PNEs that are supporting their problem. For those people, like me, the visualization is just *part* of the process. But its importance cannot be minimized. So, how do you begin this process? Let's venture on.

Creating Your **Mind Change Manifesto**

We recommend finding a journal or notebook to dedicate to this practice. Ideally, even the sight of it will evoke a good feeling. I want you to think of this document as if it holds magical powers. What you write can come true. Don't hold back. Make it the BEST! This is the place to plan out exactly what you want for the future. This is way more than a "goals list." This is a story. It needs details, images, sounds, feelings, and character development. It's also, always, a work in progress. It can be refined, fine-tuned, upgraded. It can only possess words of hope and positivity. It can have pictures, poems, quotes, cards—anything you want that makes you feel good. It can even have glitter if that's your thing.

A small caution about your wording. Our words have immense power. Remember back to our creation equation?

RUMINATION + DECLARATION = CREATION

Mind Change

This is your declaration. Words such as "don't want," "can't have," or any other words that make you *feel* bad isn't allowed. Neuro-Linguistic Programming (NLP) is the study of the way language patterns can be used to program our brains to achieve certain outcomes. Neuro refers to the brain, linguistic refers to the study of words language, while programming refers to the ability of our mind to be programmed into creating the results and behaviors we desire. The study of NLP has been a huge benefit to me in helping me change my thinking by being aware of what I am saying.

It is widely believed in the personal growth and development industry that the subconscious mind cannot "hear" negatives. Meaning, if you were to say, "I don't want to be fat," the mind only hears the "fat" not the "don't." I think it's safer to say that what we say and how we say it can have an impact on what our mind "pulls up" from our resources. The mind responds to what is being focused on. It is looking for a feeling or proof to focus on and then builds with the material it is given. The reason "I don't want to be fat" doesn't translate into "I'm fat" is because the mind understands all the feelings of being fat. It has tapped into all the resources that make this true. If you changed that statement to, "I want to be fit and healthy," your brain now has to find any resources it holds to begin to build a skill to be "fit and healthy."

People who continue to say, "I'm broke," miraculously always seem to *be broke*. My maiden name is Bolton. My father has a saying, "Well, that's just life on Bolton Blvd!" This always came after a hardship, usually financial in nature. Though I didn't realize it growing up, this mantra provided support for my belief that getting ahead in life came easy for the rich but hard for the "poor." "Bolton Blvd" signified the ancestral idea that I was stuck on this street! This was all a subconscious message that I didn't realize until later in life.

For your Manifesto, make sure that your languaging is positive and affirms what you want more of. This is not the time to restrain yourself. Your future is only limited to what you can imagine. Go big! I will ask you to restrain your "But I don't want to be let down" program and your "I'm just trying to be realistic" program and dream big. If those thoughts pop up, don't ignore or judge them, you can jot them down on a separate piece of paper. We will put them on another list described in the next chapter. This notebook is only for what you *do* want.

For some, this step will come easily. You have no problem writing your litany of wants, dreams, and desires. For others, this could prove a little more challenging. If you find yourself in the latter category, don't despair. This only means that you are out of practice with using your imagination for the good. That doesn't mean you don't use your imagination, you just probably use it to imagine all the *bad* things that could happen. Or all the ways it *won't* work out. Remember, they are both your imagination. You might as well start practicing imagining the good! It will take practice, but it is more than worth it.

Another powerful tool. When you write this, use language that indicates you *already have it*. For instance, rather than saying:

"I *want to be* fit and healthy," you would say, "I *am* fit and healthy. And with this fit and healthy body, I exercise three to five times a week and enjoy it immensely." Write this beginning part "as if," you already possess the desired thing. Here is an excerpt of my personal Manifesto from four years ago. It was in my five-year plan section. Interesting side note, **all** of these things have now manifested for me in one form or another!

I am fit and healthy, working out in the gym and lifting weights. My body is strong and can easily communicate emotions. I am self-employed and self-supporting, doing what I love and helping people all over the world. I am a speaker, an author, and an authority on mind-body wellness. I love myself in a deeper way than ever before, and I give myself the time I need.

I have a healthy relationship with food, and easily and effortlessly maintain a healthy weight. I love my body more and more. I look and feel younger because I take care of myself accordingly.

I live on a tropical island. There is plenty of sunshine, and I enjoy the outdoors regularly. My children enjoy the beach, and we are able to surf, hike, and relax in the sun. I keep a healthy work/family balance. I am surrounded by friends and people who call me higher. Opportunities are abundant. As I learn and grow, I am free to help others do the same. This comes naturally and easily.

Money flows to me, and my needs are met. Kent (my husband) and I can dream even bigger and can be partners in every adventure. My children are confident and feel loved. They are healthy and feel free to be themselves...

Again, this is just a sample of my personal Manifesto. Four years ago, I made a plan for where I was going. At the time, I was living in South Africa and had no idea how I would ever end up on a tropical island. It seemed far fetched and "wishful thinking." It was!! But the more I concentrated on clarifying *where* I was going, the paths to that place began to reveal themselves. As I said (declared) and wrote those things, I felt like I *didn't* and *couldn't* have them. But I knew that I had to make a pathway out, if even just in my mind. The Mind Change Manifesto is your pathway out! It's the first step in knowing where you are going and how you will feel once you get there!

Here are some good questions to get you thinking about what you will write:

- **Who do I want to be if I were the *best* me?** Step out of yourself and see yourself as you'd LIKE to be. This can include character traits, feelings, attributes. If you were the best person you knew, what would you be like?

- **What would I do if I succeeded in every venture?** Dare to imagine yourself as a success in everything you do. Often times, the main thing holding us back from becoming what we want is the *fear of failing*. It paralyzes us to the point that we don't even try. Try envisioning yourself as a perpetual success. How would this change your dreams?

- **How do I choose to serve others and provide value to every relationship?** Giving to others and feeling valued go hand in hand. You may give and give, but if you don't feel valued, you will only end up depleted. Create situations that will be a win/win for both parties.

- **What skills do I already possess that get me closer to attaining my goals and objectives?** It's a good idea and practice to reflect on your life with the intent of finding tools and skills that you have already attained, and then recognize how you can use those to get even more.

• **What relationships do I have that support and value my vision?** Think about people who "have your back." Even if they are no longer living, see yourself through their eyes. Notice how they already believe in you and can help you go even further.

• **If I woke up every morning feeling the best I ever have, what would that feel like?** Be specific on the visual and "feeling" of this scenario. What would you do if you woke up every day like this? How would your life change?

• **If I had a magic wand and could have anything and everything I desired, what would I have?** Don't limit yourself to tangible ways of achieving things. We will often unknowingly limit ourselves because our reality is so restricted. Allow yourself the freedom to "magically" get things. That way, you can see an unrestricted version of what you want.

• **What is great about my life now, and what would I want to make it even better?** The power of gratitude cannot be underestimated. This practice alone will make huge strides in feeling better about your life. Taking your gratitude and using it to make more gratitude is an essential "life hack"!

• **If I had a great and loving childhood, and everyone was doing the best they could, what would it have felt like?** This question holds the key to healing so many hurts and pains. Even if you believe you had a horrific childhood, give yourself a moment to see it differently. If your parents really were doing the best job they could (and they likely were, even if it was awful), find some of the wonderful treasures that you may have overlooked in the past. Write a story as if you had the childhood that you wished you had. Rather than getting bogged down with what *should have been*, take a moment to be specific about what you would have wanted. Remember, write as if you *already* have it.

These are just some of the wonderful questions that will help you build a powerful Mind Change Manifesto. Read it frequently, take planned time to envision it, feel it, touch it, taste it. Become so familiar with this plan and destination that you could recite it by memory. When you do this, you will quickly begin to notice how many things are already true and how many others are becoming true.

If you find resistance, that is okay. It can even be good. Resistance is a good indicator of investment. It's good to see what beliefs you are really invested in. Just jot it down and return back to your Manifesto. That resistance will get the attention it needs. This is an organic document, meaning it will grow and change. It's meant to be changeable. As you start to attract more and more of the things on your list, you will be able to adjust and even dream bigger. This Manifesto will also become a powerful testament to the power of your mind. In the near future, you will look back and realize how many of the things you have and your gratitude will overflow. This allows for even more greatness and growth! It's a wild and wonderful ride!

CHAPTER 14

Mind Change GPS

I am not a "journaler." Not that I haven't made countless attempts. It's just not *my thing.* That being said, it is imperative to have a place where we can store and remember our joyous times. Once you start your Mind Change Manifesto, you will become clearer on *where* you are going. Now, you need to recognize the tools you have to get there. This is where the Mind Change GPS comes into play. A GPS gives us all the tools to arrive at our desired destination. What will be included in your GPS? The "**G**" stands for Gratitude, the "**P**" stands for Positive Affirmations, and the "**S**" stands for Smiles. I will explain a little more about this later in the chapter, but having a record of "rights" will be highly beneficial to your Mind Change practice. Remember, everything is a skill. Even happiness! If our life has been in a particularly rough place for any extended period of time, it's clear that we have been "practicing" a lot less joy than we need to be. What we practice becomes perfect!

One way to practice our happiness/gratitude/joy is to record it. It's the mindset behind photo albums or Facebook feeds or Instagram accounts—a way to record all the wonderful things that happen to us. We look back on past memories and see the smiling faces, and we almost cannot help but smile now. Yes, sometimes it makes us nostalgic, which we often mistake for sadness. But actually, we are often just looking back and wishing we had been more present, aware, and grateful *then*. Keeping track of these times and reminding ourselves of all the wonderful "happiness skills" we possess is an incredible tool to utilize.

It may be of no surprise to you to note that gratitude and the "record-keeping" of blessings have been studied and researched for many years. In one recent study [1], researchers recruited 300 college students who were seeking mental health counseling at a university. The participants were studied just before they began their first session of counseling. The majority reported clinically low levels of mental health at the time. At the conclusion of the study, researchers found that the participants who engaged in gratitude activities reported significantly better mental health immediately following the study. But remarkably, they also reported benefits up to 12 weeks *after* the exercise ended.

Another gratitude study, using adults with congenital and neuromuscular disorders (NMD), showed similar findings. Compared to the control group, the participants who recorded their blessings every night reported more hours of sleep each night and feeling more refreshed upon awakening. They also reported more satisfaction with their lives as a whole. Members of the gratitude group also felt more optimism about each upcoming week and reported feeling more connected with others than did participants in the control group. Incredibly, the positive changes in the gratitude group were markedly noticeable to others. According to the researchers, "Spouses of the participants in the gratitude (group) reported that the participants appeared to have higher subjective well-being than did the spouses of the participants in the control (group)." [2]

Gratitude builds on itself. Researchers note that daily practice is superior to weekly practice. The brain changes with experience, so the more often gratitude is focused on, the more the brain learns to tune in to the positive things in the world. Though it may take a little extra effort, the payoff can hardly be downplayed. However you do decide to do this, please don't skip this step. Even if you've "tried it before," I implore you to try it again. In conjunction with the other tools you will receive in this book, you have a powerful recipe for health and happiness.

Make A Mind Change GPS

This is pretty self-explanatory. Find a journal or notebook that you can begin to record the things that make you feel happy, grateful, blessed, hopeful, euphoric, and inspired. In our modern world, this can be done in various ways:

- Written Journal: A book or binder of blank pages that you use a pen, markers, crayons, or various tools to write things down.
- Electronic Journal: This can be any word processing document system that you can write with. Google docs, notepad, Microsoft Word, Pages, etc. This is also the easiest to combine with pictures or music.
- Scrapbook/Photo Journal: Track your joyous events through pictures, stamps, or drawings. You can add a few captions here and there, inspirational quotes, cards, letters, drawings, or anything that makes you feel good. You can also add song lyrics, poems, or printed pictures.
- Combo Journal: Use any mixture of the above ideas to create your own masterpiece.

Remember, the basic components are comprised of, but not limited to:

"**G**": Gratitude - this can be daily list of things that you are grateful for. Even entering 5 items every day can be a powerful tool toward getting more of what you want in life. I do this in the evening, before bed. I think through my day and take time to record some things I am grateful for. Even on the worst days, I can find things to be grateful for. Some days, it simply says "coffee." Other days, I make a long list of things. Some things are repeated, day after day. It's all okay. Just begin to log your gratitude, daily if possible. If you miss a day, be grateful the *next* day that you were able to journal today.

"**P**": Positive Affirmations - did you know that anything you affirm will become more true to you? We *negatively* affirm all the time. "I'm such a dummy," "I can't do anything right," "I hate my job," "I'm so tired," and so on. All of those are affirmations. In your GPS, we want only *positive* affirmations. These can be little quotes, sayings, or purposeful affirmations that are being used to build you up. Louise Hay has amazing affirmations in many of her books. Also, you can find numerous affirmations online. Find these, rehearse them. Write them daily and read them, aloud if possible. You don't have to believe that these are "true" now, but things you *want* to be true in the future. Something like, "I am completely and unconditionally loved, just as I am." In a very short amount of time, you will look back at your earlier positive affirmations and realize that some of the things you wrote are absolutely true now!

"S": Smiles - this is ANYTHING that makes you smile! This can be photos, song lyrics, funny little stories, or observations. I saw two lizards having an epic battle for a female lizards' attention. It was beautiful and I made sure to write it down as soon as I was able. Even now as I write this, I have a huge smile on my face as I remember that incredible scene. You can also glue in cards, notes, letters, or other little mementos that bring a smile to your face. This will also be a vital section and a crucial part of your Mind Change practice because this will be the place you record your changed memories. If you remember before, I had an old memory of a physical abuse event with my stepfather when I was about 10. I no longer have any trace of that original memory (other than a vague awareness that it may have happened). Now, I see us going out for ice cream, and I have a cone with 10 scoops of different ice cream towering above me! I can even smell the ice cream shop and feel the cone in my hand. I wrote this memory down so that I could rehearse it and replay it any time. So much healing has come from this singular event! But my book is FULL of these "rewritten" memories.

Side note...do not let the *planning* of the "perfect journal" derail you from actually *doing* it! I am SO guilty of this. Whatever you do, just do it. Ideally, this will include happy memories from your past, things you have loved or been inspired by in the past (or present) and will also serve as something you can add to daily. Noticing the blessings about even minor topics can help you reinforce gratitude in your life. Even something as simple as gratitude for the sun streaming through the window can be a powerful practice.

Creating A Mental "Safe Haven"

Another very powerful practice that I have employed is intentionally creating a "safe haven" in my mind. Anyone who has experienced trauma of any kind can likely explain the importance of "feeling safe" in any given situation. For people who have spent any extended period of time in a "flight/fight/freeze" response, finding a calm, safe environment can be a key to healing. For this exercise, we capitalize on the knowledge that our mind doesn't know the difference between "happening now" and "already happened" if we are deeply rehearsing the memory. Having a "safe haven" that we can visit anytime, anywhere, is a valuable tool.

Inside my mind, I have created my "happy place." For me, this is an outdoor setting. For me, I can visually represent things very powerfully in my mind. For those who are not highly visual, this can be equally as powerful using the *feelings, smells, sounds*, and other details. This place is VERY real to me. I have visited it enough in my mind that I know every detail. I know what it looks like, feels like, smells like, and sounds like. I have even added in some details that I can taste. This is my happy place! I love going there. I visit it often. I cannot feel bad there. Bad feelings are not allowed. It's a very similar idea to the place that Cosette, the little girl in *Les Miserables*, explains in her song "Castle on a Cloud."

There is a castle on a cloud,
I like to go there in my sleep,
Aren't any floors for me to sweep,
Not in my castle on a cloud.
There is a room that's full of toys,
There are a hundred boys and girls,
Nobody shouts or talks too loud,
Not in my castle on a cloud.
There is a lady all in white,
Holds me and sings a lullaby,
She's nice to see and she's soft to touch,
She says, "Cosette, I love you very much."
I know a place where no one's lost,
I know a place where no one cries,
Crying at all is not allowed,
Not in my castle on a cloud.

Like Cosette, we all need a place we can go to that is exactly the way it should be. And with the amazingly creative and imaginative powers of our mind, we can have that place! This exercise will be easier for some than others, but I encourage you to keep working on it. For your benefit, I will share a description of my "happy place" for you. Remember, this is highly personalized for *me*. It may include details that you do not enjoy. That's okay! This is my place, not yours. That's the point. It's supposed to be *your* safe place. Make it as good as you want it. But feel free to borrow from mine if you like.

There is a large, crystal clear lake surrounded by mountains on all sides. The mountains are covered in all sorts of trees. Evergreens, Aspens, Willows. Out on the lake is a long wooden walkway that leads to a covered dock. At the end of this dock, I sit in a large, reclined chair. It is a large wooden Adirondack chair, with a high back. As I sit, I have a warm, soft blanket draped over my legs. It is often morning and the air still has a slight chill that lingers before burning off into a warm summer day. I hold a hot cup of coffee (or sometimes hot cocoa) in my hands. I can feel the warmth of the mug. I take a sip and savor the deep flavor. The lake is completely calm and flat. Every once in a while, an unseen insect touches the top of the lake and causes a gentle ripple on the surface. The water is clear, and I can see to the bottom of the lake. The color of the water is turquoise blue, turning a deeper blue where the lake deepens. I can hear the birds in the forest and the leaves rustle when the slight breeze picks up. I just sit, taking it all in. I take deep breaths of the crisp mountain air. The air is sweet and I can feel it fill up my lungs and cleanse my body. I am completely at peace. I am alone and perfectly at ease. I have nothing to do, nowhere to be. I can stay as long as I choose. I can smell the pine and the earthy scent of the mossy woods. I can also smell the freshness of the water. I can smell the faint aroma of a wood-burning stove in the distance. Here, I am safe. Here, I am whole.

I have never *physically* been to my happy place. But it feels as real as any other place I have been to. I'm not sure why I chose the particular details I chose. In some ways, they chose me. But I treasure this place. I visit often and have added numerous details over the years. Sometimes, I jump in the cold water and swim with manatees. Other times, I lie in the sun on the dock and take the occasional dive into the crystal waters. A dolphin showed up once! Yes, I know...there are no dolphins in lakes. But one showed up nonetheless! I often see butterflies or beautifully-colored blue jays or cardinals. Sometimes I'm wearing a bathing suit and sometimes a sweater. Those little details are flexible and change without my understanding. But some things remain constant.

The more you invest in this place and this practice, the more powerful it will become for you. Creating a place of safety and comfort is a priceless investment. I understand that some people have not had the luxury of safety in their lives. But this is something that ANYONE can create. Give this to yourself. It is a priceless investment. It will also come in handy later when you begin working through your PaNE CuRe list (more about this in Chapter 15).

Interestingly, a few years ago, I found myself in a very seemingly familiar place while visiting somewhere I had never been. Because this work is so effective with addiction, I had the opportunity to go over to the island of Oahu and volunteer my services at Habilitat. Habilitat is a drug and alcohol treatment center that deals with some of the toughest addiction cases in the U.S. It is a mandatory 24-month program, and I am honored to have worked with them. My first time to the facility, I was taken out to the "dock." As I stood at the end, I couldn't help but feel like I had been there before. I felt an instant connection and was immediately peaceful as I stood there. After a few minutes, I was shocked to realize how much it resembled "my dock" in my mind! I have no doubt that I will someday stand at the end of "my dock," somewhere in this world, and I will be flooded with all the wonderful feelings that I practice regularly.

The Dock at Habilitat on Oahu

CHAPTER 15

Curing Pain With A PaNE CuRe List

"The secret of living a life of excellence is merely a matter of thinking thoughts of excellence. Really, it's a matter of programming our minds with the kind of information that will set us free."

Charles R. Swindoll

Now that you have completed your Mind Change Manifesto, it's time to address any resistance that may have shown up. In addition, it's time to go back and take inventory of the beliefs, memories, and experiences that helped you become who you are right now. Remember, our current life circumstances, beliefs, and operations come from our internal programming. If you have tried numerous different modalities or theologies on how to "deal with" your past, you may have made the incorrect assumption that it is unchangeable. The old adage, "The past is the past, you cannot change it" comes from an inaccurate view of "the past." If the past truly was "the past," we wouldn't be currently dealing with it. But our current reality (and often our future reality) is dictated by what we already know. As much as we would like the past to stay put, where it belongs, we just don't work like that as humans. Our memory is a crucial and mysterious part of our makeup.

At Mind Change, we don't run from the past. We don't talk about it until you are (along with everyone else) tired of hearing about it. We don't ignore it and we certainly don't judge it. We *change* it! Well, technically YOU change it....we just facilitate the process. Memory is a function of the mind. How you hold memories is unique to your personal perception. Memories are the building materials you use to build your current and future realities. Ever wonder why you keep getting the same thing in your life over and over? You are building with the same logs! You may decide you are unhappy with your current environment and decide to uproot and start over, but if you bring with you the same building materials to build your new life, you basically have the same foundational problems. To change the building materials, we must first assess what they are.

We do this by listing our Past Negative Experiences and Current Realities. Take the first letters of those and we get the acronym PaNE

CuRe. I wasn't trying to be cute, but it turns out that the "cure for pain" starts with our PaNE CuRes.

Making Your PaNE CuRe List

In a moment, I will give you detailed instructions on making your list. I would highly suggest finishing this book BEFORE making your list. I will be asking you to do some things that will make a lot more sense once you have finished the book. You may experience a range of emotions when considering this task. Some people are very excited, knowing that identifying the "building blocks" of our experiences, beliefs, and realities is the first step in changing them. Others may feel like this task is daunting. First off, give yourself ample time to finish the list. You do not have to do it all in one sitting. In fact, give yourself a specific time frame each day that you will work on it. You may find that you desire to continue after the allotted time. That's fine—keep going until you are finished or feel ready to stop for the day. Otherwise, just work on it for 10, 20, 30, or 60 minutes, and then stop. Pick it back up the next day.

There will be a temptation to be very emotionally-involved in this list. As you are writing the list, it is important to remember THIS IS NOT HAPPENING NOW. You are safe. Take this opportunity to learn to be an observer. Yes, these things happened, and you have many thoughts, feelings, and sensations surrounding them. We will deal with all of that. But for now, it's simply recording them for future use.

Also, this would be a good time to have your Mind Change GPS handy. If at any point, you feel that you are becoming emotionally "triggered" by making the list, take a break and look at your GPS. Alternatively, have some funny YouTube videos handy. Whatever makes you uncontrollably happy!

Hack Your Happy

In Part 1, we learned that dopamine, serotonin, oxytocin, and endorphins are the foursome partially responsible for feelings of happiness. Neurotransmitters such as cortisol, glutamate, and norepinephrine are attributed to anxiety, sadness, and depression. We can actually "hack" our happiness!

Robert Smith of FasterEFT calls this the "Bad-Good Collapse." Think about something "bad" and then shift to thinking of something "good." If the good feelings are powerful enough, they can actually collapse the bad feeling. In reality, this is just hacking our biochemistry! Honestly, we innately know this as humans. How many of you fell down and skinned your knee as a child? A natural response of an adult is to offer a "boo-boo kiss" or a lollipop. Or they will try and make the child laugh. We know that somehow "distracting" the pain will lessen it. Oh, how right we were!! But it goes far deeper than that. I will go into this in detail in the next chapter. But for now, I want you to focus on the power of this Happiness Hack.

Dopamine is created to give you a surge of reinforcing pleasure when you feel proud of yourself or have achieved a goal. Look back at old photos of your proudest moments. Re-read touching cards or letters. Take a peek at your vision board.

Serotonin flows when you feel significant, valued, or grateful. Take a few moments to write down five things you are grateful for. Mentally or verbally affirm yourself in a positive way. You can also go for a walk or have a meal outside. Expose yourself to the sun for 15-20 minutes, which enhances serotonin production.

Oxytocin, referred to as the "cuddle hormone," creates intimacy, trust, and strengthens relationships. It's released during orgasm, and by mothers during childbirth and breastfeeding. Give a hug to someone! Also, be sure to hug yourself regularly!

Endorphins help to alleviate anxiety. Exercise often results in a surge of endorphins. Laughter is one of the best ways to induce endorphin release. Even the anticipation and expectation of laughter increases levels of endorphins. Finding several things to laugh at during the day is a great way to keep your endorphins flowing. Also, don't forget to smile. When we smile, certain muscles contract and fire a signal back to the brain, stimulating our reward system, resulting in a boost of endorphins. Even the act of holding a pencil in your teeth for a period of time can generate "feel good" chemicals.

Making The List

Now that you can "hack your happy" at any point, you are ready to make your list. Keeping the above information in mind, prepare yourself to do this by first sitting down and taking ten deep breaths. Breathing in through your nose and out through your mouth, try to match your inhale to a three-count beat (breathing in for three counts) and exhaling to a four-count beat. When you have completed your breathing, take a moment to invite your subconscious mind to bring forth the information that is needed. You can do this by verbally or mentally acknowledging that you are providing a safe and loving space for this process. When you are ready, you may record this information on paper or on your computer.

It is my suggestion that you use a notebook or journal that is specifically designated for this process. This is an organic document, meaning it will continue to change over time. It is a valuable resource, becoming a record of all the "old/former" beliefs that you once had. I cannot stress this point enough. As a self-professed non-journaler, I initially experienced resistance to this exercise. But after working with hundreds of clients, I can say that the people who *did* make this list along with a detailed Mind Change Manifesto experienced far greater changes in the long run. This is, in essence, the "before" picture when you start a workout program. Inevitably, you will need this to see an accurate view of how far you have come.

There can be no judgment here. If you begin to feel feelings of shame, blame, or grief, you need to go and "hack your happy." Come back and start again when you are ready. You can create this list in various formats, but we suggest starting from the beginning of your life. Starting from birth, or before that, if applicable, list every PNE (perceived negative experience) in your life. You will give the memory a short title and then list two or three emotions, feelings, or sensations generated by this memory. You will also rate the emotional intensity of this memory next to the title using a scale of 0-10. Zero, being you feel nothing and 10 being the worst feeling as if it's happening now (examples below). Below are detailed instructions on getting started:

1. **List any pre-birth or ancestral trauma.** These will be stories you were told, or family identities. Stories about parents or grandparents, aunts or uncles. Anything that you remember that was an unpleasant trait or story from your ancestry. You may have developed pictures in your mind or have audio recordings of the stories you were told.

Example: My grandfather was a Holocaust survivor. I would then title this memory, give it a rating and list any related feelings, emotions or physical sensations associated.

- Holocaust stories: (8)

fear, anger, rejection

2. **List any birth stories**. These will be stories around your birth or conception. Difficult labors, hardships, the difficulty of mom getting pregnant. Were you unwanted or a "mistake"? Adopted? Were you the "miracle child" they always wanted? Child of rape or abuse?

- Mother nearly died in labor: (6)

shame, blame, fear

3. **Chronologically list all other PNE's.** It may be helpful to divide your life into time periods (0-5 years old, 5-10 years old, etc.). Consider each time period and try to list 10 or more events. If you remember a specific event but do not have an emotional intensity with

it, list it anyway. Title the memory, give it a rating and list any related feelings, emotions, or physical sensations associated.

Events to include and consider:
1. How siblings & family members felt about you, how they treated you
2. School experiences: bullying, shaming, embarrassments
3. Any sexual abuse or molestation
4. First sexual experience: pornography, experimenting
5. Emotional or physical abuse
6. Religious traumas
7. Major moves, changing schools
8. Deaths of pets, pet injuries, losses
9. Any romantic relationships, especially first boyfriend/girlfriend
10. Pivotal points in life with parents, siblings, bosses, coworkers, etc.
11. Divorce, relationship breakups, broken friendships
12. Deaths, grief & loss, loss of a job, loss of health
13. All hurts, anything you felt bad about when it happened
14. All major medical illnesses, chronic illnesses, other medical problems
15. Accidents & injuries
16. Fears/Phobias, list each experience to support the fear
17. Re-occurring beliefs or mantras: "You're not good enough," "You'll never amount to anything," "You are stupid," etc.

214

4. **List all Current Realities or Core Beliefs**. This will be all the negative and/or unproductive things you believe about your life now. Examples: "I will never be well," "I don't have enough money," "I'm not good enough," "I have to earn love," "Life is hard," "My marriage is a disaster," "I'm depressed," "I am bad," "Something is wrong with me," etc.

5. **List any "unmentionables."** These will be things that you feel are too difficult to deal with, things you have never told anyone, family secrets, or things that you aren't sure really happened. For these, you do not need to add any content and the titles can be unrelated. For example, someone who remembers an incest incident but has never talked about it could list that event here with the title of "Lemonade." Lemonade may have something or nothing to do with the actual event but serves as a title for this particular memory. If you suspect something happened or that you did something, but have no memory of it, you can "make-up" a short version of what might have happened and then title it. You don't have to have a conscious construct of a memory to change it. Your subconscious mind already knows.

Be careful not to indulge in the stories. Stories are merely practice. The more we tell it, the better we get at remembering it and making it true. Remember...

RUMINATION + DECLARATION = CREATION

Once you have completed your list, you now have a starting place for Mind Change. You can now begin working your way through this list using the rest of the practicals in this book. Remember, this document can be changed, altered, and added to as time goes along. But specify short, intentional times to come back and work on this list. Do not be in continual thought about all of the PNEs of your life. Trust that if something else needs to be on the list, your subconscious mind will give it to you at the right time.

CAUTION: We do not advise trying to deal with highly traumatic events on your own if the emotional charge is very high. You may need the help of a skilled practitioner to facilitate your work on these items. Always ensure that you are in a safe, supportive environment when addressing past traumas. Do not use these methods as a replacement for skilled medical advice.

CHAPTER 16

Changing Your Mind: Rewiring Our Neuropathways

"Neurons that fire together, wire together."

Donald Hebb- Neuropsychologist

"Progress is impossible without change, and those who cannot change their minds cannot change anything."

George Bernard Shaw

We are now entering the "nuts and bolts" of the Mind Change process. Before telling you "how" to do it, I'm going to explain to you why it works. For this part, I will ask that you remember much of what we learned in Part 1. Remember back to Chapters 8 and 9 where we learned that "pain is communication." In this chapter, I mention that pain, among other things, is a feedback loop. If you hit your thumb with a hammer, you cannot *feel* pain unless the brain decides that "pain" is the appropriate response. These messages are carried along by synaptic impulses. This process creates a circular loop of communication.

What do you think would happen if we were to "de-rail" this feedback loop? If we were to intercept the messages and re-code them, do you think the outcome would be different? I'm here to tell you it is! To illustrate this, let me introduce a concept that is crucial to the Mind Change Method. In fact, this is the "magic."

Pattern Interrupt

A pattern interrupt is a term that comes from hypnosis and is also used in Neuro-Linguistic Programming (NLP) . Basically, it means to change a person's state, pattern, or trance by interruption. Any unexpected event, like a sudden movement or response, can interrupt a pattern. You may have seen this in performance hypnosis through the "handshake induction." You are introducing an unexpected or uncomfortable moment into a familiar situation, therefore causing the brain to have to reevaluate the response. You probably witness this in action on a daily basis. Have you ever derailed someone's story simply by asking a question? When they try to go back, they have a difficult time regaining their place.

I have had this happen to me many times. I have been quite amused by something that happened to me and I go to retell the story. In the beginning, I am so "in the story" I can barely contain my laughter. As I get going, someone interrupts me to clarify a detail. As I try to regain my place in the story, I realize that the situation suddenly doesn't feel as "funny" as I had previously thought! If I get interrupted again, it's even more difficult for me to find the same amount of humor. In fact, after 2-3 interruptions, I usually give up saying, "Nevermind. It was much funnier when it happened. I guess you had to be there." It may seem like I am annoyed at the interruptions, but often, I simply cannot regain the same momentum I began with and even sometimes forget the story!

We see this with children all the time. I remember a time that my oldest daughter, Cadence, was little and she fell hard and scraped her knee at the playground. It ripped her pants and she was bleeding. She let out a blood curdling cry and I knew this wasn't going to be an easy consolation. But just as I reached her, a butterfly lit right on her nose! She crossed her eyes to get a better look and was instantly unaware of her hurt knee. The butterfly remained on her nose as she slowly rose to her feet. She was ecstatic! She walked around slowly, careful to not disturb her new friend. Soon after, it took flight and we discussed it in amazement. Only after, I asked her how her knee was. She seemed confused and then remembered the scrape. She examined it, rather absently, and determined it was fine, saying it only hurt a little. She ran off to find more butterflies!

So is this just distraction? Not really. It's deeper than that. Most of the time we are operating in a "trance." Not the "cluck like a chicken" kind of thing that you see in performance hypnosis. Very simply put, a "trance" is when we are on a sort of half conscious "auto-pilot." We actually do this *most* of the time. We have "trances" for everything. It's our conditioned response to known stimuli. You are walking down the street and someone smiles at you, and without thinking, you smile back. Unless you actively engage your conscious awareness, you will have an almost automatic response to most situations. These responses are programmed by our experiences. When you Pattern Interrupt someone, they experience momentary confusion, and in some circumstances a momentary amnesia.

I know I'm not alone in the next scenario. Have you ever started to do something and after being interrupted can't remember what it was you were doing in the first place? This can cause a "state of confusion" and make you open to suggestion. We can actually *program in* another state of mind within these moments. Not only that, but with enough "interruption" we can completely scramble a well known program, pathway, or trance. Let me use another example.

Most of you reading this are probably able to recall early CDs. CDs are circular disks that have information encoded into them. If you buy a Rolling Stones CD, songs by the Rolling Stones are "engraved" into the grooves of that CD. So, when you stick it in your CD Walkman or car stereo to play it, it reads those codes and spits out Rolling Stones songs. With me so far? So what happens if one of those grooves gets a scratch in it? It skips, right? The severity of the skip depends on the severity of the scratch. What happens if you scratch that song enough? It won't play any longer.

The information feedback loop between our brain and body works very similarly. If we understand the cyclical nature of that loop, we can use it to our advantage. If we are stuck in an undesirable loop, we can interrupt it. Do it enough times and it won't play any longer! Want to experience this? Let's do a quick exercise to demonstrate.

Think of something that bothered you today or this week. For now, choose something that was mildly bothersome. Got it? Write it down on some paper in front of you. Ask yourself one question: HOW DO I KNOW THIS BOTHERED ME? Notice that we are not asking "why." We don't want the story, we want the "how you know." It may be a feeling, or a picture, or maybe you can hear the phrase or sounds. Just notice how you know. Jot down a few ways that you know below this event. Just one or two words. It can be feelings, details, or things you hear. See below for an example:

Event: Someone cut me off in traffic

How do I know: I can still see the picture of it. It made me
angry and I honked loudly.

Now, rate the level of bother that you feel. Allow yourself to be back in that situation in your mind. Close your eyes if it helps. Notice how you know if bothers you. On a scale of 0-10, give it a rating for how much it bothers you. 0 being you feel/see/hear nothing at all. 10 being as bad as if it was happening right now. If you happen to get a 0 rating, pick another event.

So now, you will have the event, how you know it bothered you, and a rating to gauge that bother.

Now, close your eyes and **be there**. For a moment, allow yourself to **be bothered.** If you see a picture, see it clearly and notice how it makes you feel. If it's a feeling, make it stronger. If it's a sound, make it louder. This may even increase the rating a bit. That's okay. When you feel like you have "engaged the bother" and begin to activate the trance, I want you to stop.

Now, open your eyes and stand up. Put your right finger on the tip of your nose and recite the alphabet. When you complete it, take your left finger and replace the right finger, allowing your right hand to drop. Recite the alphabet again aloud, this time skipping every other letter. Good job!

Now, sit back down and review your event. Ask yourself how bothered you are now. 9 times out of 10, you will not be as bothered as you were before. If some bother remains, repeat the alphabet tricks until the bother is at a 0.

Amazing, right? You are not done yet! Now think of the opposite of what bothered you. In my example, someone cut me off in traffic. The opposite of that might be that someone let me go first, or the person waited for me to go by and then gave me a friendly wave. If it's a feeling, the opposite of angry could be happy. Now, I need to ask myself to envision or feel or hear the thing that is opposite. So at this point, I would envision the person in the car waiting for me and giving me a friendly wave. I would also notice that this makes me feel happy. If it's a feeling, I may notice that I now feel happy. If I heard something, I might now realize I heard something encouraging. This becomes a powerful part of the process. Now, practice this "new experience" a few times.

Using a pattern interrupt (the alphabet game or countless other techniques), we were able to interrupt the "bad feeling trance" and replace it with something else. It's like stopping the Rolling Stones song, even though it played for so long, and reprogramming that track to play Led Zeppelin instead. Or let's look at this fictionalized conversation as another example with the communication of physical pain: (You are carrying a 20 lb dumbbell in the gym and you accidentally drop it on your foot).

NERVES FROM FOOT

Hey Brain...I think we've got problems here! Bad problems! I don't like the information that is coming through. I'm not sure what it is, but it can't be good. Red alert!

BRAIN

Got it, thanks. But you know what? My guess is that this was simply a result of us focusing our attention on something else we have coming up. I'm going to have to access the database of information to identify this message—sorry, it's classified, you'll just have to take my word for it—can I get back to you on that?

NERVES

I'm pretty sure something is wrong here. I'm telling you, this is serious!

BRAIN

Yeah, sorry. I'm almost positive that this has more to do with something else we are dealing with, but I'm not authorized to make a final decision until I've accessed the proper paperwork.

NERVES

Hey! I might not have the proper clearance for this "information" you keep talking about, but I really think this is a credible complaint, so I am going to just keep telling you about it.

(About this time, your cell phone alarm goes off. You are supposed to be ready for a conference call in 10 minutes).

BRAIN

Oh great! I've got another message coming through.

HORMONE PRODUCTION TEAM

Hey there Brain. Yeah, we just received a message from the Amygdala that we need to produce some stress hormones ASAP. Is this an accurate assessment? Are we stressed? Should we also send messages to the heart to increase its pressure? I also think it may be important to begin sweating. What do you think?

BRAIN

Okay, foot nerves, the data came back: actually, you're fine. Thanks for trying to warn us, we have it figured out. Please reduce the messages for a while. Also, you are having trouble remembering what the problem is. Hormones, yes, data shows that we were late on the last call and that did not make the boss happy. This is definitely a "all hands on deck" situation. Let's see an increase in blood pressure, cortisol, and let's make sure we stay in constant communication. This is too important to let go of. Big things at stake.

NERVES

Wait, what was I saying? It seems like I was just about to say something important. Oh well, it's gone now. I'll let you know if it comes back to me.

HORMONE PRODUCTION TEAM

Gotcha Boss. We are already on it. We will produce feelings of worry and stress to make sure the body understands the importance of the mission. This message will play on repeat until we have this solved. Go team!

Messages go up to the brain but, they also go down. This "two-way" street of pain communication holds the key to being able to intercept and completely change the transmission message.

TRANCE

A little more on the "trance" concept. We are in a trance the majority of the time. With an average of up to 50,000 thoughts per day, up to 95%

225

of those thoughts are the same thoughts we had yesterday. We then repeat those same thoughts over and over again, every day. That's a lot of practice! These have all been categorized and now are nearly automatic productions. Driving to work: Trance. Performing your work duties: Trance. Speaking with coworkers: Trance. It's the "How" you do things. Your brain already "knows how" because it does it, in some form or fashion, every day.

This is why it can seem so hard to change at times. We are keeping ourselves in the same situations, thinking the same thoughts, producing the same feelings day after day. We have a conscious awareness that we would like to be *different*, but we use the same resources to produce a different result. That is rarely successful. If we can be aware of these programs and make conscious efforts to *interrupt* those repetitive messages, then we are left open to suggestions. The brain has to recalibrate because you are introducing something unknown and unexpected into the feedback loop. Because we already have our Mind Change Manifesto, we can always suggest something in alignment with what we want for the future!

"If you think adventure is dangerous, try routine, it is lethal."
Paulo Coelho

Types Of Pattern Interrupts

There are countless types of Pattern Interrupts to help you change your mind. Below, I will list just a few. Used in conjunction with the other concepts, tools, and suggestions in this book, a Pattern Interrupt is an incredibly powerful tool.

- Say your ABCs aloud
- Play a great song and DANCE!
- Sing a nursery rhyme
- Watch a funny YouTube video
- Fake laugh
- Stand on your tippy toes and take big breaths, moving your arms up as you inhale and down as you exhale
- Do a Yoga pose
- Countdown from 300 by 3s
- Do multiplication tables
- Give yourself a big hug and say, "I love me"
- Rub your tummy with one hand and pat your head with the other simultaneously
- Do some gentle stretches
- Smile broadly and try to tickle yourself
- Draw circles on your right palm with the fingers of your left hand
- Write "I love you" in cursive on your left palm with your right fingers
- Utilize Meridian Tapping **

There really are countless ways to do this. To make it even more powerful, we will revisit the concept of Representational Systems in a few moments. But before that, I want to take some time to address Meridian Tapping.

Meridian Tapping

When I first was introduced to the concepts that were the foundation of this book and my own personal healing journey, I was using Meridian Tapping. Specifically, FasterEFT. EFT (Emotional Freedom Technique) is a very well known and effective method of dealing with negative emotions. EFT theorizes that *the cause of all negative emotions is a disruption in the body's energy system.* For those of you in the Energy Healing community, this makes complete sense. For the rest of us, this may sound a little nebulous. Though the concept of energy (not the stuff that comes out of our electrical sockets, but the "unseen force" that connects all living things) isn't new, it's still considered rather "woo-woo" in the scientific community.

Though I do believe that negative emotions can disrupt the body, we now know that emotions/feelings/sensations are actually *created* by our body. The thought that "energy," whatever that means to you, can "disrupt" our bodies still puts the power *outside* of us. Now we need to be aware of "energies" that could possibly trap us or be trapped within us. I highly respect the work of the EFT pioneers. Roger Callahan, Gary Craig, Dawson Church, and many others have made undeniable contributions to the healing community. Tapping has been met with a fair share of skepticism in the scientific community. Many doctors and psychologists have been quick to dismiss it due to the lack of research.

Dawson Church, PhD, author of *The Genie in Your Genes*, is one of the many people researching EFT as an evidence-based psychological and medical technique. Taken from the biography page of Dawson Church's site, www.dawsonchurch.com, we see the results from one of his studies.

"Church performed two pilot studies of EFT (Emotional Freedom Techniques) for post-traumatic stress disorder (PTSD). They demonstrated highly significant results despite a small sample size, indicating a robust treatment effect. This led to a randomized controlled trial, published in the oldest peer-reviewed psychiatry journal in North America, showing highly significant results. It demonstrated that 86% of veterans with clinical PTSD were subclinical after six sessions of EFT and remained so on follow-up. A concurrent study by an independent research team in Britain's National Health Service (NHS) showed similar findings, indicating that EFT meets the criteria of the American Psychological Association (APA) Division 12 Task Force as an empirically validated treatment for PTSD. An independent replication of Church's PTSD study found similar results." [1]

Clearly, EFT has been shown to help create a reduction in many stress-related conditions. The problem that persists is knowing why it works. And also, explaining why it *doesn't work* for some or becomes less effective over time. I have an EFT Master Certification and have been greatly influenced by the teachings of EFT. But I am someone who likes to understand the mechanics of something. "Trapped energy," although an attractive and reasonable concept, was not concrete enough for me. It also allowed for too much ambiguity. I needed more. After looking into

FasterEFT, NLP, Hypnosis, Positive Thought Therapy, and more...the answer became clear to me.

We needed to understand how the brain processes and stores memory, and the physiological process of stress and emotion. Once I understood this, it was easy to see why Tapping worked for many. It was the Pattern Interrupt! The tapping, thought to be "releasing trapped energy," was actually just scrambling the messages that were being played along with painful memories. Scramble them enough, the messages will no longer play! *Voila!* The science is revealed.

I still use tapping at times in my practice. But I am acutely aware that its effectiveness is simply due to the brain receiving a kinesthetic message while simultaneously trying to reproduce the known problem. They accidentally stumbled onto one of the biggest healing tools around. Yet, many still attribute it to energy. What I have witnessed both personally and professionally, is that the tapping can become another coping mechanism. People will "tap" when they feel anxious, start to feel a bit better, and then stop tapping. Granted, it's a better coping skill than some others, but it is nowhere as powerful as it could be. Knowing physiologically what is happening in your brain when you tap is crucial to long term success. When we see that tapping is simply one of many forms of Pattern Interrupt, it frees us up to be more focused and intentional in our healing.

The reason for tapping on the meridian points comes from the doctrines of traditional Chinese medicine. Chinese refer to the body's energy as "ch'i." In ancient times, they believed that by stimulating these meridian points, they could heal. The concept is similar to acupuncture. Though I believe in the notion of meridian channels, I strongly feel that the real power is in the mechanics of the brain.

Representational Systems:
The "HOW" We Do What We Do

If you remember back to Chapter 4, I briefly described our Representational Systems, better known as our 5 senses. It is through these systems that we experience our world. What we actually perceive are representations of what each sensory organ transmits to us. Each of the PNEs that you listed on our PaNE CuRe list were "input" in one or more of these systems. We all use each representational systems, but we tend to favor one over the rest. This is called our Primary Representational System. Knowing "how" the experience was recorded can be very helpful in deciding which Pattern Interrupt will be most beneficial. As a reminder, let's look at primary systems once again and the way that a memory can be stored based on each system:

VISUAL	AUDITORY	KINESTHETIC	AUDITORY DIGITAL
Pictures	Sounds	Feelings	Inner Dialog
Movies	Tones	Emotions	Mantras
Snapshots	Music	Sensations	Inner voices
Images	Speech	Touch	Logic
Shapes/Symbols	Noises	Intuitions	Processes
Colors	Dialogue	Gut feelings	Systems

So, "memory" can actually be represented in many different ways. Knowing specifically how a particular event was processed and stored can be very helpful in interrupting it. Look at the next diagram to be reminded on what happens when we receive any external stimuli (event).

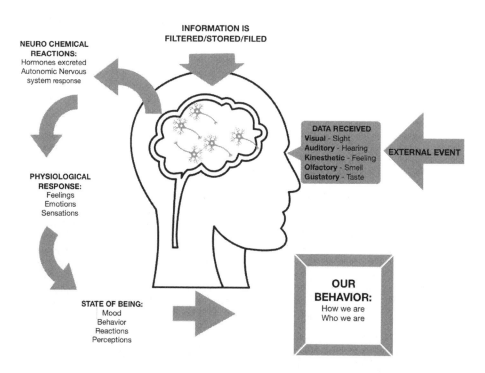

As you can see, our Representational Systems is the first set of "filters" that are used with any information we encounter. Let me explain by having you do an exercise.

EXERCISE: *Close your eyes for a moment and go back to your High School graduation. Just notice whatever comes up for you.*

For the people who stored this memory *primarily* using their Visual system, you will have noticed pictures or movies playing in your head. You may remember the color of your cap and gown, or the faces of your friends, or even your face as you sat among your peers waiting to throw your cap into the air.

For the people who stored this memory *primarily* using their Auditory system, you will have noticed the sounds of the day. Maybe you will hear the words of the salutatorian giving the speech, your name being called to come up and receive your diploma, or the applause of the audience as each classmate was called. You may remember the music, or the words of encouragement from your friends and family.

For the people who stored this memory *primarily* using their Kinesthetic system, you will experience the feelings you felt that day. The excitement or nervousness. Maybe even a little sad or even fearful. You might remember how your gown felt, or the butterflies in your stomach as your name was called. Feelings of love might be noticed as you think of all the support you had. You may even remember what the temperature was that day, or how you felt in the shoes you were wearing.

For the people who stored this memory *primarily* using their Auditory Digital system, you may hear a dialogue in your mind. Recalling each event and the schedule of the ceremony. You may be aware of the wonder you felt and the thoughts that were going through your mind on that day. You may remember the things that you said to yourself, "Be sure not to trip on stage." Maybe you recall the *knowing* that things were going to change from this point on and that you had hit a milestone in life.

Assuming that your high school graduation was not a particularly traumatic time in your life, there would be no real need to "interrupt" this memory feedback loop.   In fact, if this was a *good* time in your life, it would be beneficial to go back and spend time in this memory, noticing all the wonderful things that were there.   Interestingly enough, just by remembering this and replaying it, you can create the same chemicals and results as if it were happening to you *right now*!

Now, if we are dealing with a memory that, when originally filtered and processed, triggered a negative stress response in your body, that is something we would want to interrupt. Because, simply by replaying that memory in your mind, you can produce *feel* bad chemicals...as if it's happening *right now*!   If you identify how this memory is stored *primarily*, you can use appropriate Pattern Interrupts to scramble the message. Let me share a client story to illustrate this point and show you how I used this concept.

DAWN

Dawn came to me as a shy and reclusive woman.   She had a strong belief that she was "not good enough," "not smart enough" and a "bad person." As she worked on her PaNE CuRe list, I noticed a few domestic abuse incidents in her past.   When probed further, she described her mother being belittled and abused by her father. I asked Dawn how she knew that her mother had been abused, she said that she had heard it. I asked her to go back to one of the instances and describe it for me. Dawn said that when she was a little girl, she would often be in her room with her door closed. Behind the door, she would hear her parents fighting. A few times, it even escalated to her mother screaming in what Dawn described as pain or fear. She had also heard her Father say things to her Mother like, "You are good for nothing" or "You're so stupid" when they were fighting. It was clear to me that Dawn had input these experiences primarily using her Auditory system. As she closed her eyes, she could hear the screaming and insults as if they were being said again right there. She visibly shuddered as she replayed these phrases in her head. Knowing that we would need to address these memories using the Auditory tracks she was hearing, I decided to use an Auditory Pattern Interrupt. I allowed Dawn to get deeply in the trance of this memory, asking her to hear the screams louder and the insults even clearer. I could see her trying to make herself smaller in the chair as she relived this event. This was clearly a very traumatic memory for her. At once, I had her open her eyes and answer a question for me. "Who is your favorite cartoon character?" I asked. Rather befuddled, she searched her mind for the answer. Eventually, she landed on Elmer Fudd from Bugs Bunny. I asked her if she remembered what he said. Of course she did, "I'm a 'huntin wabbits," she said with a small smile. I quickly asked her to close her eyes and go back to the memory of her father. I asked her to hear his words and her mother's screams. A small frown appeared on her face, "I can't hear it as loudly," she said, almost disappointed. I asked her to hear it as best she could, and then, mustering my best Elmer Fudd impression, I loudly said, "I got you wabbit!" Dawn's eyes shot open and she began to laugh. I asked her to go back to the words of her Father and to notice what was there. After a longer pause, she said, "I can hear it, but just barely." At this point, I leaned in and whispered in her ear, "You wascaly wabbit!"

Dawn once again burst into laughter. When I asked her to return to the memory, she quickly responded, "I can't!" When I pushed her a bit further, she smiled slightly and said, "I can only hear Elmer Fudd!" I proceeded to further clean up and change any parts of the memory that had been stored with any of the other systems (visually and kinesthetically). Because this memory was primarily "auditory remembering," the other systems were even faster to resolve. At the end of our time, I pushed her to try and recall what her father used to say to her mother when she was a child. Of course, she instantly thought of Elmer Fudd and smiled. After that, from some of the other work we did in that session, she was able to remember many of the loving things her father and mother said to each other. In fact, she now realized that the majority of her parents relationship was actually very encouraging and affectionate. The incident she got stuck on happened to be a singular "rough patch" in an otherwise healthy marriage. But because she was stuck replaying the most traumatizing memory, she hadn't been able to recall the other things. Ironically, when she began hearing and replaying the "good" things she heard growing up, her own self image drastically improved. The next time I saw her, she looked very different. She was sitting a little taller and was much more talkative and animated.

By using an auditory Pattern Interrupt, we were able to "scratch" the track on that "CD." Also, the Bad/Good Collapse (discussed in Chapter 14) happened when she began to laugh. Dawn had been programmed early in life to feel small and "not good enough." Even though her father never said that to her, he said it to someone she loved and valued. To make matters worse, it came from someone she loved and trusted. A child

236

of 4 or 5 years old simply cannot reconcile the grossly mixed messages she was receiving. So she internalized them as a reflection of herself. Now, she is the "stupid" and "good for nothing" person. Long after her father stopped saying those things, Dawn continued to hear them! Only, it was just her hearing the recordings of past memories.

When she "hears" this over and over, it becomes a rumination. Inevitably, she begins to apologize for herself in all situations and says, "Sorry! I am just stupid." Now, she is declaring. You know what comes next!

RUMINATION + DECLARATION = CREATION

For memories that are visually held, I find it helpful to create new pictures, movies, or stories. Using new scenarios helps the client "see" a new option and can often totally destroy the previously-held visual construct. For kinesthetically-held memories, Pattern Interrupts that involve movement are recommended. Dancing, yoga, deep conscious breathing are all good options. Meridian tapping can also be utilized. Our goal is to be moving the awareness from the "old" feeling, picture, sound, to a new one. One that is "better" and that is in alignment with what they want more of in their life.

Quick note for those that are new to the concept of representational systems. People will often say, "I'm totally visual" or "I'm such a Kinesthetic." It is true that the majority of the population will have a *primary* representational preference. But it is important to understand that just because we may be holding something visually, we also *did* hear and feel things about the event. In fact, though I personally hold many memories in a visual context, my more powerful system is kinesthetic. I will usually focus on the visual construct of a memory to avoid *feeling* anything about it. When I work on myself, I will often need to change the visual construct first, and then I am able to address any *feelings* I had with regard to the memory. Remember, our subconscious mind is the smartest part about us. It will do whatever it takes to "protect" us. Even if it doesn't make sense consciously. It is important to clean up ALL aspects of a memory that are unpleasant.

If I remember an abuse scenario with my stepfather and "feel" nothing negative, but can still "see" pictures of him hitting me, I am still holding an unpleasant aspect of this memory. Remember, you will get MORE of what you hold within. If I don't want more of the same, I need to change the pictures and/or sounds that accompany these memories. The best and most effective "new pathways" will be those that have positive visual images, audio files, and feelings.

Neuro Re-Wiring

Our brain is constantly learning and adapting to new stimuli. If we are constantly finding what we already know or believe to be true, we aren't necessarily learning anything new. This is just the result of the "firing" of these well-traveled neuropathways. We often hear the phrase "set in their ways" when speaking about older people. Our brain doesn't lose the ability to adapt and change as we get older, we usually just get comfortable with what we "already know and believe." Therefore, we are simply a walking, talking product of these well worn neuropathways. BUT, if a "new" thought comes onboard, our brain is forced to adapt.

When you think about something in a different way, learn a new task, choose a different emotion, see a different picture, or take a different perspective, you are carving out a new path. Now, the brain has two possible pathways to follow. If you keep traveling the new road, your brain begins to choose this pathway more and more. The feelings created along with these new pathways become more familiar, like second nature. As the old pathway is used less and less, it weakens and eventually disappears altogether. This is neuroplasticity in action.

As we see with Dawn, her beliefs and corresponding neuropathways were formed early in life. And even though they happened many years prior, they had been reinforced and strengthened, over and over again. And thanks to the RAS (Reticular Activating System), she found proof for these beliefs over and over again. By using the Pattern Interrupt, we disrupted the messages encoded in the deep and well traveled road. This left Dawn in a suggestible state and open to a different perspective. After it was clear that the former road had become unstable, we were able to rewire or re-code the message. Now, there is a new pathway—one that has a positive and affirming message.

The goal is to significantly weaken the original neuropathway and offer an alternative route. Once that new route is traveled and the accompanying positive emotions are created, many people realize the benefit of this particular option. But it is very important to make an intentional effort to reinforce this message and travel this road daily for an extended period of time. If the new road isn't strengthened by repetition and the old pathway remains, it will be very challenging to change. You can easily fall back into old beliefs, reactions, and patterns. Lasting change comes from our daily practice of choosing which memories we replay and cleaning up anything that doesn't serve us.

Our brains are highly resilient and desire flexibility. In fact, our brain functions optimally when it is open to new possibilities and learnings. We are not only capable of changing the landscape of our lives by creating new neuropathways, our brains have highly adapted to do so. The human brain is designed to heal itself, and seems to have a deep desire to do so. Changing deeply encoded traumas and beliefs necessitates a great deal of awareness of our present beliefs and programs along with the references held by our subconscious minds. Pattern Interrupts are a great way to facilitate the process of change.

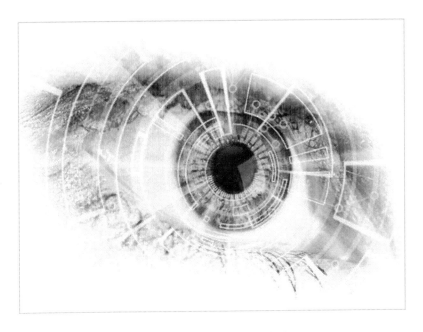

CHAPTER 17

Basic Mind Change Process

For the purpose of giving the reader an outline for how to work on themselves, I will include some helpful scripts and questions to ask oneself. For deeper or more traumatic events, I would highly suggest working with a skilled practitioner.

There are many ways to approach the way you practice Mind Change. I will go through a few of them here. For more hands-on examples and tutorials, please visit our YouTube Channel for continuously-added, free videos. At most, I would suggest spending no more than 1 hour a day on focused Mind Change work. That would be a very aggressive approach to this work. For others, it may look more like 10-15 minutes a day or 30-60 minutes a few times a week. Even if you start with 5-10 minute sessions at first, you are engaging in a powerful and intentional activity. In any case, be gentle and loving with yourself in the process.

Working Through Your PaNE CuRe List

One approach to your Mind Change work would be to work through your PaNE CuRe list (Past Negative Experiences and Current Realities). Prepare yourself for the session by taking a moment of prayer or meditation, using this time to give thanks for the ability to do this work and for the healing that will happen. Next, choose a calm, quiet area where you will not be disturbed. Set a timer for the amount of time you would like to spend. Now is an excellent time to have your GPS handy! Or if you have invested in your "Safe Haven" (Chapter 14), this would be a great time to go there and spend a minute or so indulging in the good feelings. As you do this, engage in some deep breathing. Deep, 3-4 second inhales through the nose, followed by 4-5 second exhales through the mouth. Do this 4-5 times as you are in your "feel good" state.

Pick A Memory

Either chronologically, by intensity or perceived importance, pick a memory or "problem" to work on. If it is a "problem," take a minute to notice how you know it's a problem. Allow any pictures, feelings, or sensations to surface. You may notice that one or more memories surface. If so, notate those. Even if you think they are unrelated, just trust the subconscious mind and work through what comes up. Write the title of this memory on a piece of paper in front of you. Close your eyes and "GO THERE." Notice what you notice. HOW do you know this happened? Do you see pictures? Hear voices or words? Does a feeling emerge? Maybe it's a mixture of one or more. The most important part of this is "knowing HOW you know."

Under the title, write the letters V, A, K, A/D. If you are seeing pictures, movies, or snapshots, circle the V (Visual) on your paper. If you are hearing things within the memory, circle A (Auditory). If you have feelings, sensations, or emotions arise, circle K (Kinesthetic). If you have an internal dialogue that you can hear or a "knowing" that it happened but nothing else, circle the A/D (Audio Digital). (Note: you may have one or more ways you are holding this memory. Just circle all that apply). For each letter that you circled, write 2-3 different things you notice from that category. It might look something like this:

MEMORY: Dad Yelling about my mom

(V:)   I see myself as a scared little girl, 5, cowering in the corner

             I can see Dad standing over me, face is red, eyes bulging

(A:)   I hear the scary tone of his voice

(K:)   I feel scared and helpless

(A/D:)   I deserve this.

             I am lazy

             Dad doesn't love me

             I can never be good enough

Rate Your Memory

Once you've identified "HOW" you know this event happened, notice how much it bothers you. Now you can give the memory a rating to acknowledge how much it bothers you. Something like, "on a scale of 0-10, 0 being you feel nothing at all and 10 you feel as if this is happening again right now, how much can you make this memory bother you?" Write this number down beside the title on your paper.

Don't worry if you find it difficult to select a rating. A common subconscious defense mechanism that can arise when we are working on ourselves is distraction. We get distracted by small, inane details, and we allow it to cause unnecessary friction within us. This is the mind's way of trying to "delay" the process. Just be aware of that and move forward. You can thank the subconscious mind for its constant desire to protect you and affirm that you are safe. No need to spend any undue amount of time worrying if the memory is a "2" or a "4." Just give the memory a number. Make it your best guess if you need to and be fine with that. The rating eventually comes more naturally. It is simply a benchmark for where you were when you started and used to see the progress you are making.

Now, think about or recall the problem or event in detail. Notice the emotions, feelings, sounds, and/or specific images that are present in this memory. Allow it to happen as if it's happening right now. If it's safe to do so, step into the memory, imagine yourself really there, see what you saw, hear what you heard, and feel what you felt. This is the time to make it as strong as possible because it will only last a short amount of time. This should take you no longer than 30 seconds to 1 minute. Any longer and you begin "practicing" the feelings because the feedback loop has already been playing.

As soon as you reach this place, it's time to open your eyes and engage a Pattern Interrupt. The optimal Pattern Interrupt will be one that corresponds with the Representational System that you used to most fully recall this memory. For instance, if you have a mental picture of the memory, open your eyes, and look through your GPS. Or, you can visit your mental Safe Haven. Alternatively, you can watch a quick YouTube video of funny animals. Spend 30 seconds or so in any one (or more) of these activities. The most important thing is to completely shift your focus from the memory (picture, feeling, sensation, sound) you are working on, to the Pattern Interrupt.

As soon as you are ready, close your eyes and take 2 deep breaths (3-4 second inhales through the nose, followed by 4-5 second exhales through the mouth). Notice that your breathing automatically brings you back to a grounded place. Now, go back and check your memory that you are working on. Notice what has changed. Notice that the intensity has lessened, or the picture has changed. Maybe the feeling has reduced or moved to another part of your body. Just notice what's left. Now, go to any part of the memory that still bothers you, notice how you know it bothers you, intensify it if you can, see what you see/feel what you feel/ hear what you hear...now, Pattern Interrupt again.

The Devil's In The Details

It is very important to notice the "details" of any memory/problem. The details are like the building blocks of the memory. If we change the details, the whole memory can change.

So if you notice that you or anyone in the memory is "not happy" –, we go from the general to the specific, "I'm not happy because _____," to even more specific "aspects."

So here are some potential details in this example:

"I'm not happy because my dad's tone is still rough." (This is an "audible" aspect of the event)

"I don't like the way his face looks." (This is an aspect of the experience, the "visual cue")

"The little girl is feeling sad." (Here's a "body sensation" to address)

"I'm worried he's disappointed in me." (A "future fear" to address)

"I don't like the way the room feels." (A "kinesthetic detail" to address)

"I never have good relationships with people." (A "limiting belief/past experience" to address)

And we could go on and on!

Clearing this particular experience with your father can have massive positive repercussions on a bunch of other things! For example, you start with working on and clearing the memory with your father. But as a side effect, you have a better (and less reactive) experience with your spouse later that day.

Keep Going Until It's Great

Continue this process until the memory can no longer bother you. This may happen very quickly, or it may take you the entire time that you set aside. Either is okay. Regardless of the length of time you have spent, notice the fact that you are changing and applaud yourself! "Great job, me!" Instead of simply seeing what you still need/want to change, take a moment to see how much you have already changed. Notice the good shifts your mind is capable of! Once you can no longer make the memory bother you, it's time to change your mind. If it's a picture, you may notice that the picture has already changed. The brain is amazing that way! If not, you may just notice that you can no longer find the picture, or it has gone completely blurry. Now is the time to be intentional about what we hold within. Ask yourself, "What would I have rather seen instead?" If auditory, "What would I have rather heard?" Kinesthetic, "What would I have rather felt?" Make it good, because you will get more of what you hold! In the example above, maybe the picture changes to the little 5-year-old girl, sitting on her daddy's lap. His face is gentle and loving. Notice everything that comes with the new memory. The good sounds, words, feelings that come with this new picture. Allow yourself to really be there. If anything negative or uncomfortable arises, just Pattern Interrupt and then return to the new memory.

When everything is good, and nothing can bother you about this memory, you may think you are done. But this is the point to go in and make it even better! Go back in the memory and "redecorate" a bit. Maybe now, you see daddy playing your favorite board game with you, and you WIN! Perhaps daddy is now telling you all the things you needed to hear. Maybe you are wrapped tightly in the arms of your daddy and you can feel all the love. Even better, maybe it's all of these things mixed together.

Don't worry if other memories come up during the time you are working on this one. Simply take a moment to jot them down and thank your subconscious mind for giving you more resources that have been supporting this belief/problem. You can work on them after this memory is cleared or you can save them for another time.

If you are working on a memory and find resistance, that is okay. It doesn't mean it didn't work, it only means you have a little more investment in this belief. It's likely foundational and may require one or two sessions of self-work. Take a break and come back later. You may find that the memory is now changed. If not, you will likely find less resistance when you revisit it. Just think, it probably took you many years to develop such a deeply-rooted response. Or you have practiced this memory, thousands of times, therefore reinforcing it daily. It may take you a few hours or even days to rewrite some of these events, but it is well worth it!

The first time that you rewire a memory, you may be shocked! The first few times might feel a little bumpy or awkward, but the more you do it, the more your brain gets the hang of it. At this stage of my journey, I can often change painful memories simply with the intention of doing so. My brain is so accustomed to letting go of the painful things that do not serve me that just the acknowledgment of needed change stimulates the change! Of course, some things are still very rooted in my belief system and those things take a little more work. I still utilize sessions with colleagues on a regular basis to help me clean up some of the things I am unaware of or that are particularly stubborn beliefs.

A word of caution. Though this method has been used to tackle some of the most devastating traumas, it is advised that you work with a skilled practitioner if you find that the emotional "charge" of the memory is too high. The trance of the painful memory can sometimes be so powerful that you have a very difficult time breaking it on your own. This is where an experienced professional can utilize different protocols to break that trance. This is very deep work, and it can be very beneficial to work with someone who has been trained to handle any situation that may arise. It is the ultimate goal of any Mind Change practitioner to empower the client to work on themselves eventually. Therefore, starting out with a practitioner can be very beneficial.

For more information and instructional videos on using Pattern Interrupts, please visit our Mind Change Youtube channel. This should give you a good start on how to start using these tools yourself.

CHAPTER 18

The End...Or The Beginning?

We have reached the end of this journey. I hope you have enjoyed the ride. I want you to know that this is probably not the end for you, but likely the beginning. This book is just the introduction to a longer conversation. Some of you are deeper into the conversation already, but some of you never even knew you needed to *have* a conversation!

It was difficult to know where to stop. There is so much more...there is always so much more. We are ever-changing, ever-evolving beings. Science is revealing more astounding research daily. The frontier of our minds is only barely being explored. I believe I have accomplished what I set out to do—to give you a foundation of how the mind works and also some tools to change it. But it's not the end. Even though I have found incredible healing and power with this information, I am still learning. I am always looking for faster and better ways to change and grow. I intend to continue to share that information with you.

For some people, the information contained in these pages will be enough for them to move forward and create their future by design. For others, it will be just enough to be intriguing, but they're left wanting more. Wherever this finds you, I want you to know that I am grateful that you joined me for this period of time. You are not alone. Hundreds of thousands of people around the world are ready for change. You are in good company. Or...maybe you are not ready yet. Maybe this is all a bit "too much" right now. That's okay. I've been there, too.

I want people to know that there is hope. For everyone, not just the lucky few. No matter what you have been through, no matter where you are now, it is possible to find health and happiness. It won't come in the form of a pill, or a diet, a fad, or a distraction. It won't be popular and isn't always easy. It will be maligned, mistaken, and misjudged. But the good thing is that it is within every person's reach. It will involve "letting go" of anything that does not serve you and looking beyond the mask you put on daily. No one can *make* you do it, but no one can take it away, either. A changed mind is a changed life. Only you can change your mind.

So let's keep up the conversation. Let's be the adventurers of our own destiny, the surveyors of our own mind. Let us make friends with our subconscious mind and begin to learn the language of our souls. If you need help, reach out. Read more. Listen more. Become an expert in the art of YOU. If you want more, I will include an extensive reading list. On my site, I have links for many relevant and inspiring TedTalks and podcasts. I'll do my best to keep you up to date on what I am learning and finding. In the meantime, there is no better time to start than now. Thank you for your company, each of you was thought about carefully in the writing of this book.

In closing, I would like to share with you the stories of Chinese Bamboo and the common household radish. It is said that Chinese Bamboo starts out as a hard-shelled seed. Once it is planted, it needs good soil, sunshine, and water. If at any time the bamboo isn't taken care of, it will die. After the first year, there are no visible signs of growth. Not even a seedling or sprout. Second year, same thing. Third year, fourth year…nothing. The grower just continues to water and nurture the plant from the surface. In the fifth year, the Chinese Bamboo finally peaks through and then shows miraculous growth—often 80-90 feet in six weeks! Was the little plant really dead and inactive for five years? Of course not! It was busy creating an entire foundational structure that could eventually support its enormous growth.

Contrast this to the radish; I grow these in my garden and have personally witnessed their growth cycle. Within days of sowing the seeds in the ground, little seedlings pop up. Over the next 20-30 days, they are fully developed and ready to harvest. Depending on the amount of rain and sunshine we get, it can be even faster. I can pull them up and drop in a few little seeds, and the whole process starts over again. They are easy and relatively worry-free. And they taste amazing!

Some things that you work on will be radishes. Dr. Caroline Leaf, author of *Switch on your Brain*, says it takes around 21 days for all the necessary changes in your brain to create a long-term memory [1]. Those new little memories and neuropathways need to be fed and watered. They need to be practiced over and over to build a strong root system in your mind. Other things, like core belief systems and generational mantras, may take a little longer. They may be the "bamboo" of your life. Keep watering. You will likely see a bunch of new little sprouts in your life as you apply these principles. Harvest them and enjoy. Don't forget to keep planting. Other things will reveal themselves slowly, doing the deep foundational work under the surface. Both are important.

Mind Change is important and is sacred work. Welcome to the end... and the beginning.

APPENDIX A

Recommended Resources

Online Videos

False Memories - Elizabeth Loftus
https://www.youtube.com/watch?v=PB2OegI6wvI

You aren't at the mercy of your emotions. Your brain creates them - Lisa Feldman Barrett
https://www.youtube.com/watch?v=0gks6ceq4eQ

Is Therapy Facing a Revolution? - Peta Stapleton
https://www.youtube.com/watch?time_continue=2&v=0Vu0Tibt1bQ

Science of Thought - Caroline Leaf
https://www.youtube.com/watch?time_continue=4&v=yjhANyrKpv8

How to change your limiting beliefs for more success - Dr. Irum Tahir
https://www.youtube.com/watch?time_continue=1&v=Fom14XGMFHA

Break the Addiction to Negative Thoughts & Emotions - Dr Joe Dispenza
https://www.youtube.com/watch?v=AXrdVagSjjg

How Our Childhood Shapes Every Aspect of Our Health - Dr. Gabor Maté
https://www.youtube.com/watch?v=2oicQ2xFiIc

The Body Keeps the Score: Brain, Mind, and Body in the Healing of Trauma - Bessel Van Der Kolk, M.D.
https://www.youtube.com/watch?v=53RX2ESIqsM

Is there scientific proof we can heal ourselves? - Lissa Rankin, MD
https://www.youtube.com/watch?v=LWQfe__fNbs

How Your Unconscious Mind Rules Your Behaviour - Leonard Mlodinow
https://www.youtube.com/watch?v=vcJm-y7UnLY

How to rewire the subconscious mind - Sajeda Batra
https://www.youtube.com/watch?v=_K0SP0JZPro

Healing illness with the subconscious mind - Danna Pycher
https://www.youtube.com/watch?v=erpPQDSWD0k

Book Recommendations

The Body Keeps Score by Bessel Van Der Kolk, M.D.
Switch on Your Brain by Dr. Caroline Leaf
You are the Placebo by Dr. Joe Dispenza
The Biology of Belief by Bruce H. Lipton, Ph.D
You Can Heal Your Life by Louise Hay
The Healing Code by Alexander Loyd, Phd, ND
Deadly Emotions by Don Colbert, M.D.
The Genie in Your Genes by Dawson Church
The User's Manual for the Brain by Bodenhamer and Hall
When the Body Says NO by Gabor Maté, M.D.

Appendix B

End Notes

Chapter 1: Our Beautiful Brain

1. Robynne Boyd, "Do People Only Use 10 Percent of Their
    Brains?" (Scientific America, February 7, 2008)
    https://www.scientificamerican.com/article/do-people-only-use-10-
    percent-of-their-brains/

Chapter 2: Our Subconscious Mind

1. Andrew D. Wilson and Sabrina Golonka, "Embodied cognition is not
    what you think it is" (Frontiers in Psychology, 12 February 2013)
    https://www.frontiersin.org/articles/10.3389/fpsyg.2013.00058/full

Chapter 3: "Why Am I Such A Mess?"

1. Beverly Engel, "When Did "Victim" Become a Bad
    Word?" (Psychology Today, Apr 09, 2015).
    https://www.psychologytoday.com/us/blog/the-compassion-chronicles/
    201504/when-did-victim-become-bad-word

2. Nancy Colier, "Are You Ready to Stop Feeling Like a Victim?",
    (Psychology Today, Jan 12, 2018)

https://www.psychologytoday.com/us/blog/inviting-monkey-tea/
201801/are-you-ready-stop-feeling-victim

3. Victor Frankel, "Man's Search for Meaning", (Beacon Press; June 1st 2006)

4. Merriam-Webster's collegiate dictionary, 1999,
    https://www.merriam-webster.com/dictionary/victor

Chapter 4: Thoughts = Things

1. Dr. Caroline Leaf, Switch on Your Brain, (Baker Books; September 1, 2013)

2. Lisa Feldman Barrett, How Emotions Are Made, (Mariner Books; March 7, 2017)

3. Joe Dispenza, Breaking the habit of being yourself how to lose your mind and create a new one, (Carlsbad : Hay House, 2012)

4. The Oxford English Dictionary, March 2-19
    https://en.oxforddictionaries.com/definition/perception

5. Rik, "Learning Styles: Why some children fall behind in school", April 4, 2017
    https://lifebeyondlimits.com.au/learning-styles/

Chapter 5: Memory Mis-Education

1. Elie Wiesel, "Nobel Lecture", December 11 1986.
   https://www.nobelprize.org/prizes/peace/1986/wiesel/lecture/

2. Kendra Cherry , "The Misinformation Effect and False Memories",
   March 13, 2019

3. Loftus, E. F. , "Planting misinformation in the human mind: A 30-year
   investigation of the malleability of memory". Learning and Memory.
   2005;12:361-366.

4. Garven, Sena, et al. "More than suggestion: The effect of interviewing
   techniques from the McMartin Preschool case." Journal of Applied
   Psychology 83, no. 3 (June 1998): 347–59.

5. Nadja Schreiber, Lisa D. Bellah, Yolanda Martinez, Kristin A.
   McLaurin, Renata Strok, Sena Garven, and James M. Wood,
   "Suggestive interviewing in the McMartin Preschool and Kelly
   Michaels daycare abuse cases: A case study," Social Influence Vol. 1,
   Iss. 1, 2006.

6. James M. Wood; Debbie Nathan; M. Teresa Nezworski; Elizabeth Uhl
   (10 August 2009). "Child Sexual Abuse Investigations: Lessons
   Learned from the McMartin and Other Daycare Cases." In Bette L.
   Bottoms; Cynthia J. Najdowski; Gail S. Goodman (eds.). Children as
   Victims, Witnesses, and Offenders: Psychological Science and the
   Law. Guilford Press. pp. 81–101.

7. Marla Paul , "Your Memory is like the Telephone Game: Each time
   you recall an event, your brain distorts it." Northwestern Now,

September 19, 2012.
https://news.northwestern.edu/stories/2012/09/your-memory-is-like-the-telephone-game

8. Stephen S. Hall, "Repairing Bad Memories.." MIT Tech Review, June 17, 2013.
    https://www.technologyreview.com/s/515981/repairing-bad-memories/

9. Tammy Kennon, "Why forgetting is actually good for you." The Week, August 31, 2016.
    https://theweek.com/articles/643297/why-forgetting-actually-good

10. Dr. Caroline Leaf , "The Chemical Imbalance Myth," DEC 19, 2018.
    https://drleaf.com/blog/the-chemical-imbalance-myth/

11. John D. Mayer, Peter Salovey, David R. Caruso, and Lillia Cherkasskiy, "Emotional Intelligence." February 11, 2011.
    http://ei.yale.edu/wp-content/uploads/2013/09/pub312_EIchapter2011final.pdf

Chapter 6: Trauma: It's In The Genes

1. Somatic Experiencing Trauma Institute. Accessed March 2019.
    https://traumahealing.org/about-us/

2. Somatic Experiencing Trauma Institute. Published on Oct 15, 2014
    https://www.youtube.com/watch?time_continue=2&v=nmJDkzDMllc

3. "What is TRE?," https://traumaprevention.com/what-is-tre/

4. YouTube, "Impala in and slowly out of collapsed immobility." https://www.youtube.com/watch?v=Ox7Uj2pw-80

5. Kathy Brous, "Healing Tools for Trauma." Accessed March 2019. https://attachmentdisorderhealing.com/resources/tools/

6. Van der Kolk, B. A. (2014). The body keeps the score: Brain, mind, and body in the healing of trauma. New York: Viking.

7. Van der Kolk, B. A. (2014)

8. "The Adverse Childhood Experiences (ACE) Study." cdc.gov. Atlanta, Georgia: Centers for Disease Control and Prevention, National Center for Injury Prevention and Control, Division of Violence Prevention. May 2014. Archived from the original on 27 December 2015.

9. Karol K. Truman, Feelings Buried Alive Never Die. Olympus Distribution Corp (August 28, 2014)

10. "The Adverse Childhood Experiences (ACE) Study." cdc.gov. Atlanta, Georgia: Centers for Disease Control and Prevention, National Center for Injury Prevention and Control, Division of Violence Prevention. May 2014. Archived from the original on 27 December 2015.

11. Stevens, Jane Ellen (8 October 2012). "The Adverse Childhood Experiences Study — the Largest Public Health Study You Never Heard Of." The Huffington Post.

12. Penelope K. Trickett, Jennie G. Noll, and Frank W. Putnam. "The impact of sexual abuse on female development: Lessons from a multigenerational, longitudinal research study." Developmental Psychopathology. 2011 May; 23(2): 453–476.

13. Ji J, Trickett PK, Negriff S. "Multidimensional self-perception of sexually abused girls: Factor models and differences between sexual abuse and comparison groups." Journal of Psychopathology and Behavioral Assessment. 2010;32:203–214.

14. Putnam FW, Helmers K, Trickett PK . "Development, reliability, and validity of a child dissociation scale." Child Abuse Neglect. 1993 Nov-Dec; 17(6):731-41.

Chapter 7: So We Are All Traumatized...Who Is To Blame?

1. Joshua Coleman, Phil Cowan, Carolyn Pape Cowan. "The Cost of Blaming Parents." Greater Good Magazine, December 23, 2014.

2. Bowlby, J. (1958). "The nature of the child's tie to his mother." International Journal of Psychoanalysis, 39, 350-371.

3. Bowlby J. (1969). "Attachment." Attachment and loss: Vol. 1. Loss. New York: Basic Books.

Chapter 8: Dis-Ease: Language Of The Body

1. Imre Zoltán. "Ignaz Semmelweis." 2019 Encyclopædia Britannica, Inc.. Apr 11, 2019

2. Unbelievable Facts. "10 CRAZY THINGS SCIENTISTS USED TO BELIEVE." Nov 19, 2018,

3. https://www.aarda.org/who-we-help/medical-research/published-autoimmunity-research/

4. https://www.statista.com/statistics/216632/percentage-changes-in-selected-causes-of-death-in-the-us/

5. Mayo Clinic. "Nearly 7 in 10 Americans Take Prescription Drugs, Mayo Clinic, Olmsted Medical Center Find." June 19, 2013. https://newsnetwork.mayoclinic.org/discussion/nearly-7-in-10-americans-take-prescription-drugs-mayo-clinic-olmsted-medical-center-find/

6. Schubert, Charlotte; Scholl, Reinhold. "The Hippocratic Oath: how many covenants, how many oaths?." Science.gov. 2005-01-01

7. The Regents of the University of California. "UCSD's Practical Guide to Clinical Medicine." 2018. https://meded.ucsd.edu/clinicalmed/history.htm

8. TheBrain.mcgill.ca. "Serotonin and Other Molecules Involved in Depression." Accessed March 2019. http://thebrain.mcgill.ca/flash/a/a_08/a_08_m/a_08_m_dep/a_08_m_dep.html

9. Dr. Amy Johnson. "Responsibility vs. Blame." Dr. Amy Johnson.com. Dec 15, 2010. https://dramyjohnson.com/2010/12/responsibility-vs-blame/

10. Academic Minute. "Ellen Foxman, Yale University – Cold and the Common Cold." 04/6/2015

11. Jillian Knox Finley. "Are Your Emotions Making You Sick? Science Says Yes." My Domaine. 09/23/16

12. Kathryn Hewlett. "Can low self-esteem and self-blame on the job make you sick?" American Psychological Association. July/August 2001, Vol 32, No. 7

13. Hewlett, "Can low self-esteem and self-blame on the job make you sick?"

14. Louise Hay. You can heal your body. Hay House, Inc. 1984

15. Inna Segal. Secret Messages of the Body. Blue Angel Gallery. 2007

Chapter 9: The Problem With Pain

1. Richard Parry, "Ancient Ethical Theory," The Stanford Encyclopedia of Philosophy (Fall 2014 Edition), Edward N. Zalta (ed.), https://plato.stanford.edu/archives/fall2014/entries/ethics-ancient/

2. Ozden Dedeli, Gulten Kaptan. "Spirituality and Religion in Pain and Pain Management." Department of Internal Medicine. 2013 Sep 24. https://www.ncbi.nlm.nih.gov/pmc/articles/PMC4768565/

3. Moayedi M, Davis KD. "Theories of pain: from specificity to gate con- trol." J Neurophysiol 109: 5–12, 2013. First published October 3, 2012;

4. Bultitude JH, Juravle G, Spence C (2016) "Tactile Gap Detection Deteriorates during Bimanual Symmetrical Movements under Mirror

Visual Feedback." PLoS ONE 11(1): e0146077. https://doi.org/10.1371/journal.pone.0146077

5. Janet Bultitude, "Does the brain really feel no pain?," The Conversation (September 5, 2018)

6. Danielle Dresden , "Nociceptive and neuropathic pain: What are they?" Medical News Today (2 November 2017)

7. Daniel Antoniello, Benzi M. Kluger, Daniel H. Sahlein, Kenneth M. Heilman. "Phantom limb after stroke: An underreported phenomenon." Cortex, 2010; 46 (9): 1114 DOI: 10.1016/ j.cortex.2009.10.003

8. National Institute of Neurological Disorders and Stroke. Back Pain Information Page Accessed 03/18/2019.

9. U.S National Library of Medicine. "Congenital insensitivity to pain," April 16, 2019

10. Linton. "Models of Pain Perception." Elsevier Health, 2005. Print.

Chapter 10: Will This Work For Me?

1. Richard W. Burkhardt, "Jean-Baptiste Lamarck," Encyclopedia Britannica, (Mar 18, 2019)

2. Richard W. Burkhardt, (Mar 18, 2019)

3. Luciana Lorens Braga, Marcelo Feijó Mello, José Paulo Fiks, "Transgenerational transmission of trauma and resilience: a qualitative study with Brazilian offspring of Holocaust survivors." BMC

Psychiatry. 2012; 12: 134. Published online 2012 Sep 3.
doi: 10.1186/1471-244X-12-134

4. Sorscher N, Cohen LJ. "Trauma in children of Holocaust survivors: transgenerational effects" Columbia Presbyterian Medical Center, New York, USA (July 1997)

5. "Rachel Yehuda. "How Trauma and Resilience Cross Generations." On Being (July 30, 2015).

6. Amy Ratner. "Eating Gluten One Time Might Be Enough of a Challenge To Diagnose Celiac Disease." Beyond Celiac.com, September 27, 2017.

Chapter 13: Mind Change Manifesto

1. Judith Albright, "Envisioning Success: The Power Of Visualization." Regenerate, Apr 30, 2014

2. Judith Albright, (Apr 30, 2014)

3. RF Baumeister, E Bratslavsky, C Finkenauer, KD Vohs , "Bad is stronger than good." Review of general psychology, 2001

Chapter 14: Mind Change GPS

1. Y. Joel Wong, Jesse Owen, Nicole T. Gabana, Joshua W. Brown, Sydney McInnis, Paul Toth & Lynn Gilman (2018) "Does gratitude writing improve the mental health of psychotherapy clients? Evidence

from a randomized controlled trial," Psychotherapy Research, 28:2, 192-202, DOI: 10.1080/10503307.2016.1169332

2. Ocean Robbins, "The Neuroscience of Why Gratitude Makes Us Healthier." Life, 11/04/2011

Chapter 16: Changing Your Mind: Rewiring Our Neuropathways

1. Church, D. (2010). "The treatment of combat trauma in veterans using EFT (Emotional Freedom Techniques): A pilot protocol." Traumatology, 16(1), 55-65. doi:10.1177/1534765609347549

Chapter 18: The End...Or The Beginning

1. Caroline Leaf, Switch On Your Brain (Dallas: Switch on your Brain, 2008).

What Did You Think Of *Mind Change*?

First of all, thank you for purchasing this book. I know you could have picked any number of books to read, but you chose this book, and for that, I am extremely grateful.

I hope that it added value and quality to your everyday life. If so, it would be really nice if you could share this book with your friends and family by posting to Facebook, Instagram, and Twitter.

If you enjoyed this book and found some benefit in reading this, I'd like to hear from you and hope that you could take some time to post a review on Amazon. Your feedback and support will help this author to improve her writing craft significantly for future projects and make this book even better.

I want you, the reader, to know that your review is very important, so if you'd like to leave a review, do so on the Amazon page. I wish you all the best in your future success!

Made in the USA
Columbia, SC
12 June 2020